MW01166999

# Making a Way

## EMILY DAVENPORT

iUniverse, Inc.
New York   Bloomington

# Making a Way

iUniverse books may be ordered through booksellers or by contacting:

iUniverse
1663 Liberty Drive
Bloomington, IN 47403
www.iuniverse.com
1-800-Authors (1-800-288-4677)

ISBN: 978-1-4502-5325-3 (pbk)
ISBN: 978-1-4502-5326-0 (cloth)
ISBN: 978-1-4502-5327-7 (ebk)

Printed in the United States of America

iUniverse rev. date: 10/18/10

Front cover photograph by John Steedly

# INTRODUCTION

"Emily Ann, come in the kitchen for a few minutes. I want to talk to you." I was thirteen years old and would be entering the eighth grade in the fall. This was high school, because our school had only eleven grades. I dutifully went to the kitchen and sat down at the table. Mother always did this when she had something she especially wanted to say to me. She always used both names, because that signified that it was probably very important.

"I have a question for you. What do you plan to do with your life?" Now I have to admit, I had not gotten into the future that much; what with climbing trees and singing atop the smokehouse, I stayed pretty busy. But I loved school, always did, and I still love to learn.

My mother asked this question since she was remembering that, when she was twelve, she'd been told that that was the end of her schooling and she would have to earn her keep. She had told me many times that orphans were looked down on, which I thought was mighty strange since children were not responsible for the welfare of their parents.

But times were very different in 1905, when she was twelve; through sheer perseverance, she educated herself and became a registered nurse. She told me many stories about her nursing, and my best friend and I played nurse much of the time when we were children.

One time, Mother relieved a public health nurse in Columbia for a short time, and she took me with her to visit some of the poorer sections of the city. I was seven years old. My heart was truly locked into nursing from that time on.

My answer to my mother was, "I guess I'll finish high school and become a nurse." It wouldn't be that simple. Finishing high school before I was eighteen posed a problem, because students were required to be eighteen before they could enter a nursing school.

During the Depression, there were limited opportunities for women; it was typical that if a family had money, the daughters went to college and became public school teachers. To get an education, the other option was to become a nurse and receive a stipend of seven dollars a month. Both of these avenues were for women at that time and were thought of as a community service. Those who did the work were never paid very much money. My family did not have money, but I never linked that to my nursing education, even though I could have.

Because of the delay between high school graduation and the entrance requirement for nursing, a very different type of school filled up the two years between sixteen and eighteen and set the stage for the rest of my life. This is a story about one young girl who became a nurse, only to find she had multiple talents that would lead her from one situation to another but always keep her moving forward. It's a story of growing, learning, and changing. It's also a demonstration of God's love and shows how strong faith and trust can be a positive influence on one's life.

# Setting the Stage
## 1923-1929

It was in the fourth month of the year, on the fourth day of the month, and on the fourth day of the week that I came into this world at six pounds three ounces. The more you know about me, the more you will find that it was only fitting that I should be born during the decade that is known as the "Roaring Twenties"! My birth in 1923 had another unusual aspect, because I was born in a hospital. Most babies born at that time were delivered at home. This was about the time that the medical profession believed that having a baby was a medical procedure, and that opinion didn't change for a very long time. I'm sure they probably thought it would improve the maternal and infant mortality rates, and perhaps it did. But why they ever believed that strapping a woman down to a table with her legs strapped up in the air and asking her to do what is necessary to get a child into the world is still puzzling to me after having five babies myself. Things always happen in cycles, and that cycle has now changed somewhat since many pregnant women today are choosing to have their babies at home with a nurse midwife in attendance. Ecclesiastes says, "There's nothing new under the sun," and I can believe that!

Whether it is a book or a ballgame, you have to know the characters in order to understand what the whole thing is about. The first character is my father, Roland Wheeler, who for forty-five years was a firefighter for the city of Columbia, South Carolina. Roland was born in 1885 in Newberry County, South Carolina, about thirty-five miles from Columbia, in an area settled by German immigrants in the 1700s. They were a tight-knit group of farmers who settled there as a buffer between the Indians in the North and the French settlers in Charleston, South Carolina. They were hard-working people, and all of them were Lutherans. Only Germans would have settled in the white clay and rocky soil there to make a living farming.

Roland was number six of seven children. I learned early on that he was his mother's favorite and that he was born on her birthday, February 27. The other children always knew he was the favorite, and I can remember the youngest, Claire, making an issue of that even after my grandparents were both dead. Roland was a quiet man—well, in some ways; perhaps it's better to say he was a man of few words. Of course, he was spoiled and used to having his own way all the time. He had a limited education, no more than a few years; I'm not sure how many. However, his claim to fame was that he could climb a fire ladder better than any man, no matter how much younger the man was. He still said that when he was over fifty.

He had no sense of humor, which did not bode well, since my mother was gifted with a great sense of humor. The other firefighters liked to tease him, and Mother and I did the same. My father taught me several things that have served me well. First, he did not teach me patience—far from it; he had none. When he became angry, he would screw up his face, grit his teeth, and yell so loudly that anyone several miles away could hear him. He never struck me, but he did shake me several times. What he did teach me was the value of work. You were never to stop to rest until a job was done. Your work always had to be the very best, and your word was your bond. This strong work ethic does have its limits. He would go for years without missing a day of work, always taking pride in his accomplishments even if it was a very simple task.

I grew up in a segregated society, and my father respected every person, no matter the color of their skin. His philosophy was, live and let live. He kept to himself, and I never heard him criticize anyone. Last, and certainly not the least, my father was the ultimate example of self-discipline. You did what you had to do, no matter what! You had the responsibility to be in charge of your own life and to make it the best it could be. But the greatest gift of all came from his genes. He had a fantastic memory, and my mother always said he had a memory like an elephant. I did inherit his memory, and, at my age, people often comment about it.

My father always raised chickens, and he would sit for hours at a time just watching the chickens pecking at the ground the way people today look at birds at their feeders. We always had a large vegetable garden, and when I was small, he raised flowers and even had them shown at the state fair.

When Daddy was in the house, he would sit in his rocking chair, which was comfortable for his back, and read the daily paper and *The Sporting News* when baseball was king. I don't think he'd ever played, but he knew all the statistics from as far back as his birth, I do believe. In his later years, I gave him a subscription each year for his Christmas gift. He would hold the papers in front of him for hours at a time, but I'm not sure how much of that time he was reading.

One example of Roland's self-discipline always amazed others. He smoked cigarettes, rolled his own, and smoked exactly two cigarettes each day—no more, no less. Not many smokers can do that.

Most daughters have a close relationship with their fathers, but my relationship was different. He did pay me two compliments. It was so rare for him that I still remember each one. The first had to do with a vegetable garden I had in my backyard in 1952. I had planted a row of okra. I urged him to come outside to see my garden. He did and said, "That's the prettiest row of okra I have ever seen!" Wow! I was thrilled to death!

The other compliment came when I was sixteen years old. Our family made a trip to Tennessee and Kentucky. I did all of the driving, and my father said, "You are a very good driver!" This statement came from a man who, at an earlier time, had driven a fire truck. Can you imagine how thrilled I was when he told me that? It takes so little sometimes to please others.

My father was a frugal man; however, my daughter corrects me by saying, "He wasn't frugal; he was stingy!" Maybe so, but in his day there were no credit cards and very few forms of credit. If you wanted something, you saved for it. There was no instant gratification. There was very little money flowing in those days, but more on that later. My father died in a nursing home in 1973, at eighty-eight years old.

I know very little about my paternal grandparents. I know their house in the country burned down, and they lost everything. Then they moved to Columbia to live with their oldest daughter. In Columbia, my grandmother ran a boardinghouse, and she was an excellent cook! Jacob Isaiah Wheeler died in 1932, and Rachel Loretta Feagle Wheeler died in 1935.

You need to meet Kate Stammel, my mother, who was born in Henry County, Tennessee, on July 16, 1893. She was the greatest influence in my life. Her mother was Flora Ann Hawkins McCullough from English/French descent. Her father was John Frederick Stammel, a German butcher. Flora Ann was married first to Ashton McCullough, who was a prominent citizen in the Tennessee frontier. I believe he was a Methodist preacher at one time as well. When he died, he left behind his wife and a number of children.

Subsequently, Flora married John Stammel, who was a German butcher. When I learned this, I was surprised that she, a very refined, educated lady, had married a butcher. I was reminded that a butcher at that time was a very important job; there was no refrigeration, and meat was always in demand. I felt rather bad that I had even thought the way I did. I'm not sure how old he was. Mother always said that he fought the Indians on the western frontier. However, my cousin who was into genealogy told me there was no record of his ever fighting in any battles. But he did serve, and he died in The Old Soldiers Home in Danville, Illinois, in 1922. He is buried in the Veterans' Cemetery in Danville. My husband and I visited his grave some years ago.

Mother told me about going to her father's funeral in Illinois. She was riding on the train from Columbia and was pregnant with me. She was extremely nauseated and sick from the fumes on the train. She was wearing a rust-colored dress made from a shiny fabric, and she was never able to wear that color ever again!

My grandmother, Flora Ann, died soon after her second daughter, Lizzie, was born. I don't know how old she was. Minnie was the oldest of the McCullough children and was married and had children of her own. She took Lizzie into her home and reared her with her other children. Aunt Lizzie always called her Momma.

This left Kate with her father, and he was unable to care for her. He took her to Louisville, Kentucky, to live with his sister, Emily Arney. Aunt Emily had been married at one time, but no one seems to know what happened to her husband. I have run into this before. In the early years of this country, if a marriage did not work out for whatever reason, the husband just left, and no one ever knew what became of him. I guess it was one of the family secrets. This happened to Aunt Emily, and the same thing happened to one of my father's sisters.

During all my early years I heard about Aunt Emily. You must know by now that I was her namesake. She was almost totally blind from cataracts, and she was a very strict German lady, especially in regards to child rearing. Mother said that Aunt Emily would braid her hair so tightly that she felt her eyes would pop out. There were so many things she told me, things like this, that happened because of her blindness.

Kate was a pretty little girl with honey-colored hair. She was also exceptionally bright. She attended school in Louisville. It was a small school with only two teachers, Miss Lizzie and Miss Linnie Bach. Both were "old maids," totally dedicated to teaching children. What I remember most was their penmanship. What beautiful script they had! It was a very far cry from the handwriting of today, very far!

The girls wore dresses to school but wore aprons over them. Each child had a slate for writing in class. Mother said the boys always cleaned their slates with spit, and the smell was just terrible. They had small tin lunch buckets they carried to school each day. When she would tell me about the school, she recalled that they learned poetry much of the time. She remembered so many verses. When I was growing up, she used to recite all these verses she had learned in school over and over, and I still do the same today.

This section of Louisville was settled by German immigrants. Most of them knew one another, and they did many things together. They drank a lot of beer and would sit around talking and drinking beer until late at night. They had neighborhood parties. Mother said sometimes she would be sent to the "store" with an empty bucket and bring it back full of beer for all those gathered for the party.

Things went on like this until Kate was twelve years old. She had always wanted a beautiful girl doll with real hair. At Christmas that year, one of her uncles gave her the doll of her dreams. Shortly thereafter, Aunt Emily took the doll away from her and told her she was too old to have a doll. She emphasized that now that she was twelve, it was time for her to work for her keep. Her life changed drastically. Aunt Emily explained to Kate that she was an orphan and would have to make her own way. There would be no more school for her.

Mother told me she would go live with some distant cousin, or the like, and clean house, cook, and help with the children. She was treated like a servant. The children of the home would go ice skating, and, of course, Mother was not allowed to go. On one occasion, she told me, she put dirty dishes in the oven so she could at least go outside. You could tell she was still thinking like a little girl who wanted to play. It was very hard for her to accept these arrangements, but, of course, she had no choice.

When Kate was about fifteen years old, she went to stay with a different family. There was a young son in the family, and he became smitten with Kate's beauty. The two fell in love and wanted to get married. The boy's mother told Kate she was trash, low-class, certainly unfit for her son. She also told her to leave immediately.

At the time, Kate's half-brother, Ashton McCullough (everyone called him Mack), was working for the telephone company, stringing wire near Columbia, South Carolina. Mack went to Louisville, picked up Kate, and brought her to Columbia, where she went to work for the telephone company as well. The telephone company was a place where women could work, and it was considered all right for them to leave their homes.

I don't have a timetable for these years, but Kate had always loved to learn and did well in school. At this point, she decided she wanted to become a nurse so she could continue her education. She went into nursing at the Columbia Hospital School of Nursing. The training of nurses involved study and work in the hospital, as well as very strict regulations. They were furnished food and housing.

One story Mother told me took place when she was working night duty in the hospital as a student. Students were supposed to sleep every day after working the night before. Mother was caught going out instead of sleeping, and she was punished for the violation. She had always been on her own, and this made her very angry. She quit nursing on the spot and went back to work at the telephone company.

But the education bug had grabbed her, and, later, she went back into nursing at the South Carolina Hospital for the Insane. This hospital had an affiliation with St. Elizabeth's Hospital in Washington, D.C., where the students received their practice in a general hospital.

Kate said she felt she had found a home at the state hospital. There were parties and dances for the patients, so she had friends, even if they were different. Finally she had a social life.

I think about this situation often. At that time, when patients were admitted to the state hospital, they knew they would be there for life. There were no medications like we have today, and I'm sure lots of them would be on the street in today's world. So it wasn't as bad as you might think for the patients. Of course, some were very bad, and Mother liked to tell me about her experiences. But she was happy there.

The way my mother talked about nursing, I thought it was the most wonderful job in the world. She was so proud of her experiences. Later, she was one of the first public health nurses to be hired by the City of Columbia.

Kate graduated from the State Hospital School of Nursing with the highest grade of any student who had graduated up until that time. When I looked at her textbooks later, I found them to be about the same as the ones I studied when I went into nursing in 1941. Not much change took place in nursing until after World War II. She had educated herself, and she never stopped learning. She was reading world history when she was a patient in a nursing home.

My mother reared me to be strong, because she said I would need it to be a woman in a man's world. She made sure I was well educated. I was given violin lessons at a young age, later piano lessons, and later voice lessons. It was very interesting to me that though my mother was a wonderful cook and seamstress. When I would ask her to teach me either skill she would say, "You will be in my way." I think she wanted me to marry a rich man and run a large household, but I missed that. She gave me cultural things instead.

My mother set quite a pattern for me. She read all the time, and she loved history and politics. Since my father didn't talk much, she would talk to me. I remember her coming into the bedroom when I was small to tell me about something in the headlines of the paper. One morning she came in all excited and woke me up to tell me, "Wake up! The Lindbergh baby has been kidnapped!"

Kate always regretted that she did not have her mother to rear her. But she did her best to prepare me to face the world and be successful.

Kate Stammel Wheeler died December 5, 1975, from complications brought on by polycythemia, a blood disease that causes an overabundance of red cells in the blood. She is buried in Elmwood Cemetery in Columbia, South Carolina.

It was a cool spring day when my father drove his Model T Ford to the Columbia Hospital to bring my mother and me home. I am sure it was because I had a frugal father that we had a Motel T. Most families did not own a car at all. Not only that, but we owned our house as well, while most residents rented places to live. The hospital was on the corner of Hampton and Harden Streets. We drove west on Hampton Avenue, turned right on Main Street, and headed north. Soon we were at the junction of Main and River Drive, and we turned left onto River Drive. After driving a long block, we turned left again onto Columbia Avenue.

This portion of Columbia Avenue was a wide, unpaved street, but it was only one block long, and at the end there was a wooden fence. At this point, the street became one lane and was named Barrett Street. It, too, was only one block long. Traffic was scarce so few people had cars, so it did not pose any problems. The fence was built by the railroad and kept automobiles and people from going into the deep cut behind the fence. At the bottom of the cut was a railroad track. When a train went through the cut, all the houses on the block received a good shaking, ours included. Columbia Avenue continued north on the other side of the cut. There was a fence on that side also.

Our house at 1010 Columbia Avenue was a four-room, white clapboard house with green trim. There was a brick coping about 18" to 24" high enclosing the front yard, with a brick pillar on each side of the concrete walk. There were no paved sidewalks along the street. The grass was neatly trimmed, and there was shrubbery at the base of the house. The house had a front porch that was narrow on one end and wide on the other. On the narrow end hung a swing, and in the wide area were two large rocking chairs that were constructed at the state penitentiary by the inmates. They did excellent work. We had a back porch also, but later it was enclosed to make another bedroom.

In the living room, which I thought was large when I was a child but it probably wasn't, there was a fireplace with a coal grate. I remember well the family coming to our house for Christmas dinner. One time in particular I stayed on the floor in front of the fire and slept. Everyone thought that was unusual since I was always running, laughing, and talking to everyone. The next day, Mother discovered that I had chicken pox and a fever, so I slept all that Christmas.

The bedroom was at the front of the house. I had a bed in one corner, and my parents had a bed in another corner. Next to that room was the dining room with the table and chairs pushed into a corner. During the winter months, this was the "activity" room.

We had a coal stove for heating, and we stayed in there around the stove. It was where I did what little girls did while Mother sewed and Daddy read the papers. On a table was our first radio. Again, my frugal father was early in getting a radio. We listened to *Amos 'n' Andy* every night, as well as other programs.

The next room was the kitchen, and it was different from the others in one specific way. Houses were built on brick piers—pillars, we called them—and as the house aged, the floor began to sag; so our kitchen dipped down in the center. It definitely needed two more brick pillars to support the middle of the room. Placed along the wall, starting from the door to the screened porch, was an electric refrigerator. It wasn't very large due to my frugal father. Others in the neighborhood had ice boxes and bought ice from the ice wagon pulled by mules, that came around often. Next to it was a single sink. On the back wall were a window and a kitchen cabinet, where Mother made hot biscuits every morning. She made German dumplings and all kinds of other goodies every day. In the corner was another small coal heater. On the other side wall in the corner was a ten-gallon crock. Sometimes it was filled with shredded cabbage that was aging; after it stopped fermenting, it would be packed into jars, so we had wonderful sauerkraut. In the winter, Daddy would make raisin wine in the crock, which meant that he would sit and stir and stir over and over every night until it, too, would be put into containers for storage. In the corner next to the dining room was a pantry built across the corner at an angle. On that wall was another window. The table and four chairs were in the center of the room, with one end of the table a bit higher than the other and dipping down somewhat in the middle. The bathroom was located off the back porch. It was a comfortable little house. None of the houses on our block were large; in fact, one house across the street didn't have but three rooms.

The lot at 1010 Columbia Avenue was narrow but very deep. We had a very narrow driveway that led to a single-car garage. The fenced backyard was spacious, and that's where our black bulldog, Bingo, stayed. The yard was covered with clotheslines filled often with sheets and other clothes waving in the breeze; Lou, our black washwoman, did the wash every Monday.

Beyond the backyard, running from the narrow gate to the garage wall, was a large chicken house. Residents were allowed to raise chickens in the city at that time. My daddy always had lots of chickens. He preferred Buff Orpington chickens, because they became large in a short amount of time. Fried drumsticks and thighs, my favorites, were absolutely delicious. My daddy would sit for hours just watching his chickens pick at things in the scratch pens he had built for them.

Through another gate was a large vegetable garden on one side; on the other side of a wire fence was Daddy's flower garden. I don't know when they moved into the house, but later he did not grow many flowers. However, we always had gorgeous yellow daffodils and other spring flowers that came up each year.

My parents were married by the Lutheran pastor of St. Paul's Lutheran Church in Columbia, where they were members. My parents took me to St. Paul's to be baptized when I was three weeks old. There was never any question about attending church. Our family was there each and every Sunday throughout my young life.

Columbia was growing in population, and a new church, Reformation Lutheran, was built closer to where we were living. Soon the three of us joined Reformation. My parents were not charter members but joined soon after. At that time, the church was just a little wooden building with cane-bottom chairs. The Reverend Wynne C. Bolick started the church; he was a dynamic pastor, so the church grew rapidly. In the late twenties, we built a fairly large church. The women had a Ladies' Aid Society and a Missionary Society, and Mother was very active in both. The women held fish fries and other functions to raise money to meet the needs of the church. At some point, the large body of the Lutheran church did not want the individual churches to raise money anymore; rather, every member should tithe and give freely to meet the needs of the fledgling churches.

If you remember, our street had only one block, with three houses on the north side and five houses on the south side. None of the houses were large. Five of the houses were rentals, so there were people moving in and out often. Three of the houses were very important to me because of the children who lived in them. The smallest house on the block was across the street from us. After the Thompsons moved out with their four boys, Mr. and Mrs. Raines and their daughter, Libby, moved in. Libby was two years younger than I.

On the east side of us lived the Bouknights and their two young girls, Mary Elizabeth and Sophia. The two older children were by his first wife, who was the present Mrs. Bouknight's sister. The girls were Mrs. Bouknight's own children. But it was plain to see Mrs. Bouknight didn't like children very much.

The most important family of all to me was the Flemings. They had three children: Ambrose, who was the oldest, Iverson and Ella Ruth. Ella Ruth became my lifelong friend. She was two years older than I, and Iverson was four years older.

For many years, I kept trying to remember the earliest happening in my memory and one that I could actually document. Finally, I did remember, and it had to do with Ella Ruth. She was small, and never in her life did she weigh a hundred pounds. She had very small bones and looked much younger than she was. Children started school at six years of age, but no one believed that Ella Ruth was six years old; she was assigned to the pre-primer class, which was much like the preschool of today. Birth certificates were not created until 1915, so a birth in 1927 may or may not have been recorded. Home births often went unrecorded.

So Ella Ruth went to pre-primer at Logan Grammar School in Columbia. At school they did all kinds of crafts, the same as they do today. One day, Ella Ruth came home with a clock she had made out of a small vanilla wafer box. I was standing by the gate to her backyard when she came to show me the little clock. This is very clear in my mind today, and since I know she was six years old, I know that I was four years old. This does document my earliest memory.

Oh, how we did play! Iverson would pull Ella Ruth in his wagon with me pedaling behind them on my tricycle. They had a large yard, and we would go round and round faster and faster, and sometimes Ella Ruth would fall out, but never mind; she was up and climbing back in the wagon. Iverson and Ella Ruth would climb up the Chinaberry tree in their yard and urge me to join them. However, the first limb above the ground was too high for me to reach, so they would jeer at me because I couldn't get where they were. I was average or perhaps a bit larger than most for my age. But Ella Ruth, as I told you earlier, was like a little "monkey" the way she could climb the tree.

Iverson and Ella Ruth would climb on top of their garage and urge me to come on up. The first time I was able to climb up on the garage, they jumped down and left me up there, and I couldn't get down. Boy, they loved that, with me standing on top of the garage crying. When I finally got down, I ran home and told my mother about it. She said what she always said about these kinds of problems: "I'm sorry about it, so you just stay home. If you don't go over there, they can't tease you." Of course, in a short while I was back at their house. This teasing must have happened at least a hundred times, but I always went back for more.

Ella Ruth and I made playhouses over and over again. Mr. Fleming had a little room at the back of the garage where he stored his tools, and we were allowed to play in there. We would stack six bricks to make a stove, and we would sweep the dirt floor over and over. We would find pieces of wood and make a table and chairs. After we had worked hard all day making the playhouse, we were through with it. The fun was in the making.

Iverson's birthday was on May 13, and Ella Ruth's was on May 14. One year, they had a birthday party for the two of them together. We did a lot of fun things, but what I remember most is pinning the tail on the donkey. I did not win the prize, so I went home mad and disappointed. In a short while, I went back to the party so I wouldn't miss the ice cream and cake.

Ella Ruth and I had small china dolls about two inches tall. We took scraps from my mother's sewing and made clothes for them.

We would take a scrap of cloth about one inch wide, wrap it around the doll, and put a pin in it. Each doll had lots of pretty outfits. Ella would sit on one side of the front concrete steps, and I would sit on the other. We would take the dolls to visit each other, and we would talk for them.

The Flemings had a large front porch that was straight across the front but went around to the side of the house where they had a swing that we enjoyed. The front of the porch was especially important to us. We liked to sing and dance, and would do all kinds of performances. The older couple who lived on the other side of the railroad cut would listen, and sometimes they would clap for us.

We lived not too far from the Confederate Soldier's Home. Of course, there were no more veterans around, but there was a number of widows still living in the home, and I guess you could say that we took our singing and dancing "on the road." Even today, old people enjoy watching children sing and dance.

In the spring, when everyone was planting flowers or a vegetable garden, we wanted to do the same. The house where the Rains family lived had a garage that was located on the far side of their lot, and it opened onto the street. Beside the garage and inside the railroad fence was a small triangular piece of ground. It was very grassy, dry, and hard, but for several years Ella Ruth and I dug and dug all day to make a garden. We would plant seeds, and they did come up, but by then we were tired of gardening.

As we got older, we would dress up and play "grown girls" and have paper rolled up like cigarettes. Neither of us ever really smoked. We would put on high heels and drape clothing around us, even a hat, and then we would strut around make-believing that we were rich. Neither of us was ever rich, either. But there was one make-believe that did turn out for us. We played nurses often, and both of us became registered nurses.

Oh, how we enjoyed roller skating! I had blisters on my feet many, many times as a result of skating. There was a steep hill on Price Avenue, quite a distance from our homes. Several times, Iverson would join us, and we would go flying down the hill, watching to make sure no cars could hit us. Once I fell down and hit my head on the curb of the street, but no one got into a panic about it. They helped me up, and off we went. I was the youngest and less experienced, but I was determined to keep up.

During the summer months, Mr. Fleming, Iverson, Ella Ruth, and I would set up a card table on the side of their porch and play Rook and other card games that Mr. Fleming taught us. The others would always beat me. Maybe that is why I don't like card games to this day. Sometimes Mr. Fleming would take us swimming at one of several lakes open to the public in the Columbia area at that time. When they visited Mrs. Fleming's mother in Irmo, twelve miles away, they would take me with them. I called Ella's aunts the same as she did.

There was a streetlight between our two houses, and at night the other children would join us under the light as we played Pop the Whip, Red Rover, Hide and Seek, and jump rope. None of us wore shoes in the summertime, and we had stubbed toes frequently.

I've told you that Mrs. Bouknight did not like children. There was an empty lot between our house and theirs. She had flowers and shrubbery against the fence, about twenty feet from the dirt sidewalk. Along the sidewalk, cedar posts had been put down as a border. Of course, when we were playing, someone would often run across the border onto the grass. Mrs. Bouknight drove nails into the posts, hundreds of nails, and left them protruding about an inch, hoping to keep the children off the grass by damaging their feet. We just stepped over the posts.

Mr. Raines's job took him out of town frequently, and when Mrs. Raines became pregnant, Ella and I were very confused about how she could get pregnant. We knew it took sex to have a baby, but we could not figure out how she could get pregnant with her husband out of town. We thought you must have sex every day to have a baby. I was older when I learned that having sex once could result in a pregnancy.

The Flemings attended the Methodist church, and Ella Ruth wanted me to go to Sunday school with her. After much persuasion, my mother said I could go. On that Sunday, I was very excited as I got dressed up. Her teacher was soft-spoken and very nice to me.

She asked, "Would you like to join the class?" I gave a resounding, "Yes!" She asked for my phone number, which I have never forgotten, so I told her: 4994. Later, she called my mother, and that was the end of that.

On the wall of the railroad cut was a very, very narrow ledge, and the boys in the area would come to "walk the cut." It was so narrow that it was necessary to put your abdomen flat against the wall, spread out your arms, and ease your way along. Iverson and Ella Ruth wanted me to "walk the cut" with them. I was afraid, but they begged and begged until I agreed. I was afraid, but I wanted to do it. They finally convinced me. With great trepidation, I did make it across, after slipping a couple of times. Of course, Iverson and Ella Ruth finished, no sweat, but I inched my way across. I was proud that I could do it, but I never wanted to do it again.

Mother had a charge account at Mrs. Wylie's grocery store, and I would take my friends to the store and get candy or whatever we wanted and charge it to Mother. She never said anything about it. I sort of did what I wanted to do. Mother was always reading or sewing, and at that time children were safe and free to do whatever they wanted to do.

By the time I was nine years old, I was coming up with ideas of my own. I was not dependent on the older children to make all the decisions. My mother had a friend who lived in Lamar, South Carolina, and you will hear more about her later. She was a musician, had never been married, and lived with her parents. Ella Ruth and I had decided that we wanted to take a trip somewhere. I suggested that we go to Lamar to see Lucile. We got paper and pencil—there were no ballpoints yet—and wrote to Lucile. It went something like this: "Dear Lucile, can me and Ella Ruth come down there to see you?" Well, she promptly telephoned my mother, who knew nothing about the letter. They worked it out so that Ella and I went by train to Lamar by ourselves and stayed a week.

What a week it was! The Lamar area grows tobacco, and it was harvesting time when we were there. Each morning, their cook prepared breakfast for us, and we went to the tobacco barn, where they were preparing the tobacco leaves to be cured. There were black women called "stringers" and others who handed the leaves to the stringers. The tobacco leaves were brought to the barn on sleds drawn by mules and unloaded. Then the leaves were handed to the stringers, who tied them on long wooden sticks to hang on the racks in the barn. All the black workers enjoyed us two ignorant girls, and they let us hand the tobacco leaves to the stringers. We were so proud that we were working and having fun at the same time. We didn't see Lucile, but we were fine and happy. After we worked, our hands were covered with the sap from the plants. We couldn't believe how thick it was. We had to scrap it off and then use other kinds of solutions to remove it. Remember, I was nine years old, and Ella Ruth was eleven years old. We went back the next summer and stayed two weeks, and we talked about it until Ella Ruth died in 2007.

In 1932, the Township Auditorium was opened in Columbia, and it could seat three thousand people. Everyone was thrilled about it. There was a big production for the opening that was put on by the city parks. Each park was assigned a month to represent, and Earlewood Park was assigned the month of June. Our leaders chose to have a Tom Thumb wedding as our program. I was a bridesmaid in this production, and all I can remember is that I wore a long blue organza dress.

By this time, I had been taking violin lessons for about a year and piano lessons for two years, as I remember. I had been in two plays at school: one was on Colonial America, and the other was about Mozart.

As you can see, I was not at home very much of the time. I spent all my time with my neighbors. Ella Ruth and I were always the best of friends.

# Big Changes
## 1929-1934

In 1929, as the country was moving merrily along in the Roaring Twenties, it was unprepared for what would come next. I started school at Logan Grammar School in September of that year. Columbia had an excellent school system, and they had a staggered entrance. Children started the first grade in September or January, depending upon when they reached their sixth birthday. I started the first grade in September, because my sixth birthday was in April. The grades were referred to as low or high to denote the change during the school year. My first year I was in low first and moved to high first in January 1930.

I was very bright; due to my mother teaching me things at home, it was decided by those who decided these things that I should skip low second because I was ahead of most other students. You will learn later why this became significant during my grade school years.

It was Black Thursday, October 29, 1929, when prices collapsed on the New York Stock Exchange. This was the beginning of the Great Depression. It was a terrible time for the United States. Many wealthy people lost everything, and many of them committed suicide. There were no jobs, and many of those who had jobs were laid off. Ella Ruth's father lost his job with the railroad. My father had his job but was paid in script several times. Prices went up, and there were people who did not have food to eat, so there were long bread lines during these troubled years. My family was fortunate; we had chickens and a big vegetable garden all the time. There was just no money available for any purpose. People had to mend clothes and just make do with what they had. Often they shared with others. Everyone seemed to be more concerned about others during this difficult time.

Franklin D. Roosevelt became president in 1932 and set about getting the nation back on its feet. All kinds of federal programs were put into place to provide jobs, and the workers were paid with federal money. The Works Progress Administration (WPA) was a very important one. This program built schools and improved some that were already built, as well as other public buildings. Another was the Civilian Conservation Corps (CCC), which built parks and improved others. They paved walks and streets to and from the parks. There is no way to tell you all that these programs accomplished.

My father had some money saved in a building and loan, I believe. He and Mother were concerned that this money might be lost. My father had been planning to retire, so Mother encouraged him to decide what he wanted to do and perhaps to use the money rather than risk losing it.

You would think that all these things would be enough, but there were many more very important changes taking place, especially for me. Miss Gittman, who was a public health nurse in Columbia, took a three-month trip to Europe. She was my mother's friend, and she had known her since her nursing days. Miss Gittman asked Mother to work for her while she was on her trip. Of course Mother agreed to do it. What made it special was that sometimes she would take me to work with her. We visited the poorer homes around Columbia, and that just reinforced my desire to be a nurse. It was the only thing I had ever thought about. My mother was an excellent nurse, I learned later, and there weren't many other job opportunities for women until after World War II. This was in mid-summer of 1930.

My Aunt Belle McCullough, who was married to my mother's half brother, was living in Spartanburg, South Carolina. Her sister, Della Patterson, had delivered a baby boy, her ninth child, on April

14, 1930. A few days later, she died of a heart attack. It was necessary for someone to take the unnamed baby and rear him. My Uncle Mack was very ill and had been for quite a long time, so Aunt Belle couldn't take the baby. She asked my parents if they would take the unnamed baby, and they agreed. My mother had always wanted another child, so she was thrilled. The baby had stayed in the hospital for four months, and he weighed only twelve pounds. He was a very poor-looking baby. In August 1930, my parents took Ella Ruth and me to Spartanburg to get the baby and bring him home. I don't think my daddy was as thrilled as the rest of us. But you could never really tell what my daddy thought about anything. My mother named him Eugene Patterson Wheeler. Eugene was for my father, and Patterson was his family name.

Logan Grammar School was lovely. Just by looking at it from the outside, you could tell it had been well constructed by people who took pride in their work. In today's world, so many buildings seem to be just thrown together; bridges collapse, tunnels flood, and highways have been built with inferior concrete. But Logan, built in 1913, stood firm and solid. Inside there were no lockers; instead, each classroom had a large cloakroom. I should know, since I was sent there as punishment on many occasions. I, even then, was always talking when I should have been listening. Later, I would find that on my children's report cards was written, "Talks too much!" What's the old saying—"the apple never falls too far from the tree"? So, what could I say?

In one instance, my classroom was on the second floor, and I was sent to the cloakroom. I went over to the window, looked down, and thought perhaps I could jump out the window. It was not a suicidal thought; I just thought it would get everyone's attention. There was a large bush right under the window, and my thought was that the bush would break my fall. But when I thought about how it would hurt to fall into the bush, I cancelled the whole idea.

School started in September 1930, and I went straight to high second grade, skipping low second. Our school had two playgrounds: one on the right side at the back, which was the girls' playground at recess; and one on the left side at the back, which was the boys' playground. I know that must sound strange to you, since many schools have now cancelled recess altogether.

When school was over in the afternoon, all of us who walked together met at the gate and started home. One girl, and I even remember her name, Frances Dent, was in my class. Her father worked for the Ford dealership in Columbia, and he came in a new car to pick her up after school each day. All of us were jealous that she had a ride while we had to walk.

We had a wonderful school! In the upper grades, we had a fulltime teacher who taught us penmanship every day. We had a music teacher who had a rich contralto voice, and she would always sing to us. We loved the "Big, Brown Bear," and she loved to sound like the bear. Miss Bessie Davis, the librarian, read to us about the Jewish people who were in Egypt, about Moses and the plagues and the forty years the people wandered in the desert. I have remembered these stories all my life.

I don't want to forget to tell you that we also had an art teacher. What a wonderful school, with all these extra things that the kids enjoyed so much. We had the usual reading and arithmetic as well. When I was in the low sixth grade, my arithmetic teacher was Miss Black; schoolteachers were not married at that time. Anyway, we were adding decimal fractions, and I was always in a hurry, so I made frequent mistakes. Miss Black kept me after school day after day, and she told me she would do that until I learned to take the time to add my figures and get the correct answer. I don't remember how long it took, but I can tell you that I know how to add a column of figures. I'm not very fast at it, even now. Where's that calculator?

Gene went by the Wheeler name until he finished high school. During the summer months, two of his siblings would come and visit us, so he knew his biological family. After high school, Gene wanted to join the air force; he was underage, but Mother signed the papers for him to enlist. It was then that we all found out that Gene had not been legally adopted. All the legal work had been done, but it cost $400 for the adoption to be recorded with the state. My father saw no need to complete the adoption.

When Gene received his birth certificate, there was no name on it. Then he ceased to be a Wheeler by changing his name legally to Gene Patterson. He married Patsy Poole, now deceased, and they had three daughters. Gene retired from the air force after serving for over twenty years.

During the early thirties, my father was exploring possibilities for his retirement. Another fireman told him about a farm that was for sale in Lexington County at a very good price. It had 160 acres and a bold stream, which could be dammed up to create a small pond. Everyone in Lexington County had a small pond for their livestock. If you remember, I told you about the German people who came to South Carolina and settled in the rocky, white-clay land, which was very difficult to farm. The land in Lexington County that my father was interested in was sand land and very poor for farming. The midlands of South Carolina are on the fall line. Millions of years ago, the sea covered about half of the state. Of course, it wasn't a state then. In Lexington County, the lower part of the county is sandy, but the upper part is red clay. Where you have good land you have prosperous people, and where the land is poor, the people are poor and struggle to make a living from the land. My father wasn't looking to farm and be prosperous; instead, he planned to have a sharecropper to farm the land, and he would have his big garden and all kinds of animals and his beloved chickens, as well as turkeys and other types of fowl. They do well on any kind of land. So the purchase was made.

There were no structures on the property. First my father built a huge barn, and then he built a tenant house. It had four rooms with front and back porches. It costs $400 to build. A well was dug, and a pitcher pump was attached. The well had an abundance of water, even though it was only thirty feet deep. Then he built a smokehouse and fenced in a chicken yard for the tenants.

About a year or so later, after Mother drew the house plans, my father had a large brick house built for us. It was, and still is, the only brick house in that part of the county. It had three bedrooms, a large living room, and a separate dining room. It had a large, open front porch, but the smaller back porch was screened. Then he built a smokehouse and a chicken house and fenced a yard for his chickens. We did not have indoor plumbing, so we had a cute little house out back.

Our house was built on what Mother called "Gooseberry Ridge," and over and over they tried to sink a well for us. The well digger went down two hundred feet but could not find water. For many years, we hauled our water from the tenant house, and the little pitcher pump just kept on pumping.

Finally, my father built a dam for his little pond. But, would you believe, after many, many years of ample water, we were now in a dry cycle? We never had any water in our pond, but the lovely, sturdy dam is still there today. Maybe someday there will be more water.

All of this activity took about four years. Now it was time for the Wheeler family to move to the country. The year was 1934, and the war between Germany and England was going full tilt. Our country was not in World War II at that time, but we were aiding England in her fight against Germany. Many young American men were enlisting, and some went to England to help fight there. Due to this situation, the fire department would not let my father retire at this time.

So on July 12, 1934, we made our move from 1010 Columbia Avenue in Columbia to Route 4, Lexington, South Carolina. Mother, Gene, and I would be there all the time, and my father would come on certain days and occasionally spend the night. The fire department changed shifts each week, one week days, one week nights, so that determined when my daddy would be home. I guess you could say that he was an early commuter in a Model A Ford on an unpaved road to Columbia.

We gave up city living, and that was a change. We had no electricity and no telephone, but we did have kerosene lamps. We had a kerosene refrigerator that made ice cubes but no running water; and, as I told you, we hauled our water in a trailer. I learned to drive so as not to slosh the water out of the ten-gallon buckets. Let me remind you that the Model A was a stick shift, and I was very proud that I could drive it better than my parents. Mother was forty-one years old when we made all these changes.

I have never understood why she was willing to give up city living and take on a new life that was foreign to her. She was always trying to improve herself, and perhaps it was for the adventure; perhaps it was the challenge involved. These are the same characteristics that are so strong in me.

The kitchen was the center of activity at our house. My mother was a fabulous cook, and with all the fresh, thick cream and butter available from our cow, the food was out of this world! We had the usual wood cook stove that had a warming closet at the back of the top and a water reservoir on the side. In the winter, each of us would take warm water from the reservoir in a small pan, put it on the table, and take our baths right there. Even when the weather was very hot, Mother still cooked on the wood stove and even canned all kinds of vegetables. On one kitchen wall, we had a table with two buckets of water and a dipper. Everyone drank water from the same dipper. On another wall, we had a two-burner kerosene stove that we used occasionally.

Mother made all my dresses. When chicken feed came in cloth sacks during the Depression years, she made my panties and many other things out of "chicken feed sacks." I do believe she could do anything. All this time my father was outside doing his thing, and I, too, was doing mine: sometimes climbing, sometimes collecting bugs, beetles, butterflies, or whatever was available. I often said, "My mother was a wonderful seamstress, and she was an expert cook, but she never taught me to do either one."

# *High School Days*
## 1934-1939

Oh, how I loved living in the country! What a wonderful place it was! There were so many new things to see and do. Even though I was only eleven years old, I had more or less always been on my own, because my mother was always trying to improve her education and spent her time reading books. I was free to do whatever my friends and I decided upon. You remember the letter we wrote to Lucille in Lamar? Even then, when I was nine years old, my mind was always working. I wanted to know the why of everything, and I haven't changed yet.

My father bought us a 1928 Ford automobile, which he drove on his trips back and forth to work. The country people referred to them as "drug-up" roads, because they were scraped frequently. Now you have probably figured I would want to learn to drive! My mother taught me what I hadn't learned by observation. In South Carolina, one could get a license at age fourteen. This was due to boys driving tractors on the farms. Anytime we had a car, I would be driving somewhere. I was twelve or thirteen years old. Now before you talk about the risk involved, let me remind you that there were few cars; and when I would drive to Lexington, I could put the accelerator to the floor going down a long hill and get forty-five miles per hour. There wasn't too much danger. When I was a little older, I got used to handling the car, and I did other things. For example, I would drive as fast as I could and then slam on the brakes so the back of the car would slide around on the sand! I really thought that was great fun!

During basketball season, we would have practice after school. I would ride home on the school bus, get the car, and drive back to Pelion. After practice, I would drive all the other girls home. Just recently, one of my classmates reminded me of the times I took her home after practice. My family had much more than the others who lived in that area, because my father had a job and the others farmed the poor sand land.

In the country, we had a mule, a cow, several hogs, and cats that had moved into the barn before we moved into the house. Nearer to our house we had chickens, lots of them, and turkeys, guineas, and bantams. My daddy had a large garden, which took all of his time when he was there during the day. He always worked very hard; I don't think he ever knew an easy way to do anything, and the hard work seemed to be what he enjoyed most.

Our first tenants were Eschol and Inez Price, and both were reared on farms. Eschol took care of the animals at the barn, and we took care of the fowl. Remember, this was 1934, at the height of the Great Depression. Eschol had been working at a day job, but it disappeared when the crisis occurred.

Mother milked the cow twice a day. I have no idea how she learned to do it; she had never lived on a farm. But she always amazed me. She knew about everything and could do almost anything. In the winter, when it was very cold, she would get up early, go to the barn to milk the cow, and come back with a bucket of warm milk, which she strained into a large bowl and put in our refrigerator. She would get warm water from the kettle on the stove and put her hands in the water to warm them.

We had a large area behind the barn fenced in where the "bold" stream ran. The stream was never bold enough for the pond that was built, but it was bold enough for the hogs to enjoy wallowing in it. There was a fenced area from the lot outside the barn down to the fenced area where the stream ran slowly. Later, when friends visited,

I would take them from the barn all along the fence and back, which was quite a long walk. I never tired of doing that walk.

There were lots of trees, mostly pines, but some oaks. Oaks in Lexington County were officially black oaks, and they never grew more than eight to ten feet high, so everyone referred to them as Black Jack oaks. The trees were just beautiful in the fall; their leaves turned a vivid red, with some yellow and some orange. But one species of oak did grow into large trees, and they were the ones I climbed. When I went off to college and would come home on a visit, I always climbed the large oak in the chicken yard and sang so everyone in the county could hear me. Our nearest neighbor was a half mile away. Sometimes I would straddle the gable on the smokehouse and sing so loud that the Taylor family said they could hear me—so you know it was a very quiet place to live. Oh, what fun I had! I was never, ever lonely!

You would think that by living in the city with all the conveniences of electricity, telephone, running water, and an inside bathroom, the inconveniences of living in the country would be difficult for us. It was quite the contrary. My mother seemed happier than she had ever been; and just like I did, she sang all the time as she went about her housework. When she wasn't singing, she was quoting poetry to me.

In the summertime, with no air-conditioning, it was so hot that I would put my pillow at the foot of the bed right by the window to sleep. When the moon was full, I could look out the window and see the large fields of corn standing tall in the moonlight. I can close my eyes and still see that scene, which was just one of so many wonderful things to remember.

My father wanted to plant everything. We had a large strawberry patch that produced abundantly, asparagus, and all the usual Southern vegetables. He planted peanuts, corn, sweet potatoes, and red potatoes. He planted cane to make molasses and chufas for the hogs to eat. The chufas would be fenced in and the hogs turned loose inside the fence. What a time they had rooting up the nuts on the roots of the plant! The first year we were there, my father grew about four acres of wheat, and we took it to the mill in Lexington to be ground. Each farmer was given a specific acreage from the government for planting cotton. That, too, was during the first year, so we had a small field of cotton but none after that year.

There was only one thing I did not like: butchering day. In the late fall or early winter, we would butcher one of the hogs. The neighbors would come to help, and it was an all-day affair. My mother made lots of sausage, liver pudding, and corn meal mush. These things were divided among those who helped, and there was always plenty to go around. How my mother learned to make those extra things, I have no idea, but she did a great job. The hams and shoulders were taken to the freezer locker, where they were cured before being put into our smokehouse. We did not do any smoking. The thing I disliked about butchering day was the smell of the fresh meat and the grease that was involved. To keep from being involved with all the activity, and to avoid the fresh smell on butchering day, I would ride home with my friend Aletha on her school bus and spend the night. I'm sure those working at our house didn't mind that I wasn't around asking too many questions, which I am sure I would have done. I did enough of that the first time I witnessed all that was involved in changing a hog into pork!

As soon as we moved to the country, we visited Holy Trinity Lutheran Church in Pelion. Pelion was the small town close to where we lived. I think the population, at that time, was two hundred people. In the center of the town was a crossroads with a blinker light. The church was about three blocks from the blinker. The first Sunday we attended, I was surprised that the men were sitting on one side of the church and the women on the other. There was no rule about that in 1934, but I was told later that that had been the custom early on, and it just continued. The church had an old pump organ, which a lady played in a jerky way. I don't guess she knew how to play and sustain the notes so the music would be smooth. The pastor served four churches, so each church had two services a month. One service was held in the morning, and the other was held in the afternoon. There was some sort of arrangement when there was a fifth Sunday in the month.

The second year we were in the country, Ellis Corley and I were confirmed. The pastor taught us the Lutheran Catechism and prepared us for the service. There were only about forty people who attended church, so we did not have a Sunday school at first. Later, if there were any children there, they went to the back of the church, and all ages were together. It was the best we could do.

Now, about the organ. Later, when I was in high school, I played the organ for services, and I was so thrilled; I could vary the pumping, sustain the notes, and make it sound like a pipe organ. Really, it sounded pretty good and it wasn't jerky at all.

The school situation was quite different, too. There were no low and high grades in Pelion, so the principal had a decision to make. I had finished low sixth in Columbia, so he could start me in the sixth grade or move me up to the seventh grade. He decided to put me into the seventh grade, so I skipped another half year. There were only eleven grades in the South Carolina schools at that time, and in Pelion grades one through eleven were all in one building. All the students took the same subjects in the same grades year after year. Grades eight through eleven were classified as high school. If a school did not have the minimum number of students, which was seventy-two, it was closed, and the students had to attend another school. Fortunately, we had seventy-three students at that time. There was no penmanship teacher, no music teacher, and no frills at all. But I did have a typing class and a bookkeeping class that was counted as a mathematics class. My last two years in high school, I worked in the office during my free period and helped Mr. Ergle, the principal.

We did not have a cafeteria, but we did have a one-room "Soup Kitchen," we called it, where we could also buy a hot dog and a cold drink. Funniest thing: the soup was so good, and, to this day, I have not tasted a hot dog as good as those.

We did have basketball for boys and girls, and I loved that. I played guard, but we didn't win any games, as I remember. But I sure enjoyed the practice, as well as the games, and all the community turned out to see us get beat yet again. My number was four, and my boyfriend was number four on the boys' team.

Lexington County had a track meet each spring. We worked hard to be ready. We were allowed to enter three events. My senior year, I entered high jump, running broad jump, and the fifty-yard dash. The girls could run only fifty yards then. I am still proud to say I won first place in each of the events I entered. I still have the clipping from the paper. I have often wondered if I could have run marathons like women do today; if so, how well would I have done? One thing's for sure: I could really move up and down the long halls at the hospital. Perhaps my training at Pelion High School prepared me for that. You think?

The second year we lived in the country, we had a boarder. Lucille DuBose, who lived on the tobacco farm mentioned earlier, came to stay with us. Lucille finished Coker College, an upscale college, with a degree in music. When times are tough, music is one subject that gets cut from the school curriculum. Lucille had been a school teacher so she was in need of a job. She felt that if she could board with us, she could find enough pupils to teach to provide some income. The agreement was for her to pay forty dollars a month for room and board. Mother gave up her bedroom for mine, and I slept in the hall. Well, it could have been an okay arrangement, but it wasn't. Lucille started teaching me piano and voice and started teaching Gene piano, though he was only four years old. She told Mother that this teaching was for her board. Of course, Mother was depending on the forty dollars a month to help with the groceries and other living expenses, but Lucille won. She complained because neither Gene nor I would practice the piano like she thought we should. When she started on me, I would have an itching fit. Lucille, being an old maid, of course knew all about rearing children, and she never failed to tell Mother what she did wrong. That situation was for one year only, and it was very hard on all of us. Needless to say, she wasn't my mother's friend after that. Gene and I sure were glad to get our freedom back!

We were the only family in that part of the country that had a radio. On Saturday night every week, several people from the area would come to our house to listen to the *Grand Ole Opry* until midnight. Mother really didn't like the music, but she didn't complain. I guess she figured it was better than having Lucille quarreling with Gene and me all the time—or better than me having one of my itching fits!

Soon the high school days were over. We chose our superlatives, and I was chosen the prettiest girl in the class. This was no great thing since we had only five girls in the class. I had another honor: I was the salutatorian. My average was in the high eighties, so there was no big competition there, either. I did get a sportsmanship medal. The school just happened to have one on hand, and we had no money to buy me two medals. I accepted the sport medal and thought it was really more appropriate for me anyway. Our graduation was in May 1939.

There was evidently a lot of talk and discussion that went on behind my back either during my last year of high school or during that summer. Mother had learned that I could not get into nursing school until I was eighteen years old. If you remember, I finished high school a year early, because I skipped two half grades; I was only sixteen years old when I graduated. What would they do with me for two years? My Aunt Belle and my mother had many conversations, I am sure. Aunt Belle and Uncle Mack had a son named Alexander, who had attended a two-year school called Textile Industrial Institute, which was located in Spartanburg, SC. It was a work school, and every student who went there worked at a job either at the school or in the city. When my father learned he could send me to college for $14.00 a month, he was ready to listen. Later, we began the process of getting me enrolled in the school for the fall session.

They accepted me in the fall, and I was assigned to work in the kitchen; remember, working in a kitchen was new to me. But Mother made me the blue and white uniform the kitchen and wait staff wore when working. I was very proud of the uniforms and began to get excited about my new school.

# College Days
## 1939-1941

I want to take the time to tell you about this school; there were similar ones in the United States and Canada. Textile Industrial Institute was located in the cotton mill district in Spartanburg. You could see about four textile mills from the campus. The school was started by Dr. Robert Camak, a Methodist theologian, in 1912. The purpose of the school was to provide an opportunity for mill workers to complete their high school education. Of course, those who were going to school would also be working, so a pattern had to be worked out to take care of their schedule. The high school was gradually phased out, and when I went there in 1939, there was just one high school student; she graduated in 1940. Then the school was a junior college. Its name changed twice after I left. First, it was Spartanburg Junior College; later, it became Spartanburg Methodist College, which was more appropriate.

As I have told you, everyone worked. There were two people assigned to each job. There was a Section A and a Section B. I'll explain my first year and you will understand. Section A would work for two weeks, and then the person from Section B would work two weeks at the same job. When I worked, I took only two courses, and when my work partner worked, I took four courses. It reminded me of an orphanage since we lived together, worked together, and went to school together. We became very close to each other.

We had cows that the guys milked, and others who worked on the grounds. We had four shifts for the work in the kitchen and dining room. A number of the students earned their way fulltime and had jobs in the city. They would work fulltime for two weeks and then go to school fulltime for two weeks. It worked out well for all concerned. I feel that I was fortunate to have attended the school at this time, because after World War II, those in the service had the advantage of the GI Bill to pay for their education; the total work program, as I knew it, was abandoned.

I want you to remember that the textile mills moved from the North to the South to take advantage of cheap labor. Mill workers came in from the farms to take the mill jobs, so most of them were poorly educated. When Dr. Camak saw this great need, he set out to help, and he did. However, where I lived in Columbia, I was not near the cotton mills, and none of the children who went to my schools were from the mill section. They were often referred to as "lint heads." Due to the cotton lint in the air, and the high humidity in the mills, the lint stuck to the heads of the workers.

The first few months at Textile were very traumatic for me. The girls and boys were very different from the ones I had known, and many of them had come from mill villages and knew one another. Some of the students' tuition was paid by the Methodist church where they were members. We had very strict social rules since our school was coed. A boy and girl could sit on the lawn together after supper in the summertime, or, in the winter, they could go to the gym to sit and talk. There would not be any smoking, drinking, or dancing. We never entered another room in the dorm without first knocking. If a boy and girl wanted to go to a movie in town, they had to have a chaperone, and that had to be a faculty member. We learned to respect one another and to behave in a very proper way. Well, this threw me for a loop at the beginning since I had been pretty much doing whatever I wanted to do.

For the first few months I was there, I threw up after supper each night. The matron said she had never seen anyone so homesick. The adjustment was extremely difficult for me. The girls were all nice to me, but I was like a square peg in a round hole. Everything was so different that it was overwhelming. Many of the other girls knew one another, and they were different in so many ways. Most of them came from poor families, and the way they approached everything was different from anything I had known. One of the girls taught me how to iron clothes and became a dear friend and sort of a mentor. They all knew how to cook and sew; they had come from large families where they had to do these things. You remember that no one had taught me. There was so much love, respect, and caring in them toward one another. This was something I didn't know about either.

We didn't go home often, but we did go home for Christmas. After all my struggles, I decided that I was not going to stay at Textile. So I packed everything I had and told the girls I wasn't coming back. My mother met the train, and when I told her I had been sick, she said, "Tomato soup will fix you up." Later, she asked me why I had packed my trunk to come home for Christmas. I was scared, but I quietly told her I wasn't going back to Textile. I told her I wanted to live at home and go to Carolina, the University of South Carolina. Well, as usual, she knew exactly what to say; most times it hurt, but it was necessary for me to be told.

She said, "I hope you have somewhere to stay, because you do not have a home here anymore. You're almost a grownup now, so you just have to make your own way. Your daddy will not pay for you to go to Carolina." Pelion School had not yet let out for the holidays when I arrived home. The next day, I went to the school to see my friends.

Another girl was working in the office where I had been working. I watched the basketball practice; my position had been taken by someone else. I can't begin to tell you how I felt. I was a little girl in a "no man's land." My boyfriend was in the service, so it didn't take me long to realize that I was a lost girl. I didn't belong in Pelion anymore, and I couldn't stay in Columbia, so I was completely confused and had no place to call my own. I sat for long periods on the porch swing. When the sun was up, I climbed up my favorite oak tree in the chicken yard, but I could not solve my problem.

I'm pretty smart, you know, so gradually it sunk in that I had no choice but to return to Textile. When my two weeks of vacation were up, I was ready to return to school and realized what I had to do. This was the first giant step I took to start rearranging my life. I put a great deal of effort into changing myself. I watched the other girls, and I wanted to be more like them. They told me about their churches, what they learned, and how they lived. I was really interested, and I noticed the influence their religion had on their everyday lives. I had been a dutiful Lutheran, but I had not learned what they had. We had Bible class each year at the college, and I tried to pay close attention to what was taught; I hoped it would help me to be better satisfied with myself.

The second year I was at Textile, a new girl came in who had been a cheerleader at her high school. Until then, I hadn't known what a cheerleader was. She was pretty, well dressed, and quite a charmer. I was jealous of her. Everything was so easy for her, not like my struggle. I was very nice to her, however, and gradually we became good friends. I found I was no longer jealous of her at all. Then I realized that this was no trick. If you try, you can make yourself do whatever it takes to like or love someone else, and it doesn't take anything away from you. What a wonderful fact about positive living I had just learned! That experience has stayed with me throughout my life.

I was seventeen years old when I made a commitment to God: "I will spend the rest of my life trying to make life better for others." It was many years before I realized the impact that Textile had had on my life, and I have never forgotten my vow to God.

I worked in the kitchen both years I was at Textile. The first year I worked 12:45 PM to 4:14 PM and helped wash all the dishes from dinner by hand. Then we prepared the food to be cooked for supper. I think we had potatoes every day. We would sit in a circle with a large pot of water in the center, and we would peel the potatoes and throw them in the pot. It wasn't like work at all, and we enjoyed being able to sit, peel, and talk. The talk part was the most interesting.

The second year, I worked from 4:15 PM to 8:00 PM, and we actually prepared and cooked the food. I remember that it took twenty-eight cans of salmon for us to have salmon croquettes for supper. These were the regular #2 cans. After supper, again we washed all the dishes, pots, and pans. I guess you could say we sort of washed our way through school.

I was on a partial scholarship, but we had some students on full scholarships. They worked a regular workday for two weeks, and their work partner worked two weeks. Sometimes one of them would have to work late, and I would prepare supper for him or her when he or she came into the kitchen.

One young man often came in late for supper, and I would get his supper for him. One night, I talked to him for quite a while. I asked him his name, and he said, "R. B." I told him that wasn't much of a name; I thought he should have more. He said, "Why don't you name me?" I thought he should keep his initials, so I thought for a few minutes and then said, "What about Raymond Bruce?" He liked it, and from then on he was Raymond Bruce—to me, anyway.

R. B. was on a full scholarship and worked at Belk-Hudson Department Store in Spartanburg. Each time he came into the kitchen, we spent a lot of time talking to each other, and soon he was my boyfriend. We courted according to the rules, but we continued to see each other in the kitchen.

Once when he came in, he told me that Belk-Hudson was going to have a party and that he would like me to go with him. The school was very strict for the girls but not for the boys. We really wanted to go to the party together, but we couldn't think of a way to do it. I remembered that when I was nine years old, I did something like that. It was when Ella Ruth and I went to the tobacco farm.

I had standing permission to visit my aunt in Spartanburg, so I decided I would go to a hotel and get a room for the night. We would go to the party, and I would spend the night at the hotel and catch an early bus back to school. R. B. would go home and spend the night with his friend.

When the day came, I went to a hotel downtown and rented a room for the night. R. B. and his friend picked me up, and we went to the party. After the party, I returned to the hotel, only to find two policemen waiting for me. I very calmly told them the story. One guy said to the other, "I have a daughter, but she's never tried anything like this!" They told me I could not spend the night there. What I didn't know was that Camp Croft had been reactivated, several thousand men had arrived, and some women had followed the soldiers to the Camp. Later I realized why they were disturbed about me, a single young woman doing what I did. But I was not afraid at all.

R. B. had waited downstairs to make sure I got to my room alright. I picked up my small bag and went downstairs. I told him what had happened, so we started walking along Main Street. We walked and walked and walked. We walked to the edge of town, where there was a large billboard. Everything was very quiet, and we felt sure the policemen were watching us. We put our things on the ground and stayed there until daylight.

Later, I caught the bus and calmly walked back into the dorm. I remember I was very sleepy. The police must have called the school and verified that we were students there, and the next thing I knew, I was in the dean's office. This happened in the spring, and I was restricted to the campus until the end of the school year. I didn't mind the restriction, because I didn't go off campus anyway. I was afraid they would tell my parents, but obviously they didn't. The whole thing was punishment enough for me.

R. B. and I continued to be sweethearts until I went into nursing in Columbia and he went into the military during WWII.

In the summer of 1941, I was home in the country. I climbed the big oak in the chicken yard and sang and dreamed of becoming a nurse. Being alone has never been a problem for me. I learned when I worked at Educational Television that this is creative thinking, and it is a big part of organizing the written word. While I was having a lovely summer, things were quite different in other parts of the world.

Adolph Hitler's Nazi military was marching through Europe, taking over every country they entered. Thousands of Jews and others considered undesirable were loaded into trains with nothing but the clothes on their backs and taken to concentration camps. At the same time, every night for months war planes were conducting a blitz over London in an effort to break the will of the people and conquer England.

Italy, under the dictator Mussolini, joined forces with Hitler, which spread the war over more areas, even into North Africa. At this time, the United States was not officially in the war, but many young men went to Canada to enter the battle for Britain. The general public was well aware of what was taking place in Europe, and much work was going on behind the scenes to prepare the United States for war; it was beginning to appear inevitable. Most people felt it was only a matter of time before we became part of the fight.

My mother had completed her nursing education in 1917, at the South Carolina Hospital for the Insane, and she wanted me to go to school there. However, our family doctor insisted that Mother enter me into the Columbia Hospital School of Nursing, a general hospital. After receiving his valued opinion, Mother agreed. So it was that I entered training there on September 11, 1941.

# Nursing School
## 1941-1944

The Columbia Hospital was organized by the King's Daughters in 1892. It became the Columbia Hospital of Richland County in 1909. The hospital was located on the southwest corner of Hampton and Harden Streets. When I entered nursing, the wards of the very old hospital were still being used. The wards included Men's Medical, Men's Surgical, Women's Medical, and Women's Surgical, which was a twelve-bed ward. During the twenties, the east wing was built. At the far end of the block was the hospital for black patients. During the three years I was there, the Guerry wing was completed, and it replaced the oldest buildings. The hospital for black patients was remodeled, and a corridor was added; it became part of the white hospital. A new building for black patients was built on the southeast corner of the complex. In the center of all this was William Weston Hall, the nurses' residence.

I remember well the day my mother and I entered the residence. We entered a large parlor that was nicely furnished with couches, chairs, tables, and a piano. On one side was a large fireplace, and on the other side was a cabinet radio. As we came inside the building, we were greeted by some nursing students, and I received my room assignment. There were some large rooms with four to six beds, but I was assigned to a room with two beds. Willette Lucas was my roommate. The matron on duty was at the parlor door, where she could watch who came and went and who did this and was not supposed to.

What do you do with about fifty girls who just came in off the street to turn them into efficient, caring nurses? First, they must learn the rules for living in a complex with the other girls. Nurses, at this time, were trained on the medical model. This is very significant, because this model meant we would work and work hard. In fact, it was very much like the military. Everyone was very strict with us. The times we worked, ate our meals, slept, and/or had free time were clearly defined. The rigid rules were necessary for the tasks before us. We had to be punctual at all times. When we were to eat, we were to be there at that time, no other. I had just come from a church college, so I was used to strict rules, but some of the girls had a very hard time learning to conform to the nursing school's demands. When I was at Textile, there was no smoking, no dancing, no entering another student's room without knocking, and a general respect for everyone.

The nursing dorm was quite different, even though there were rules. Some of the girls had been in the workplace, so they walked around smoking. They would walk up and down the halls in bra and panties, and sometimes no bra! I guess you could say that my education began before I had even attended one class. Many times I was glad that I had been disciplined at Textile and realized the need to conform to rules.

We had to know a few things before we could go into the hospital. One of the first courses we took was hospital housekeeping. One of the first things we were taught was how to wash a pitcher and glass. Miss Mary Lou Corley taught us, and she was very strict. When you were finished washing these, you poured water into and out of them, and if the water clung to the glass, it wasn't clean—and you had to do it over. We learned how to make a bed properly, and we practiced over and over to be sure the corners were correctly done. After we had done all these things correctly, we were to walk out of the "room" and look back at the bed, bedside table, and chair to see how they would look to someone just entering the room. If you moved anything, you always put it back where it had been before.

We learned how to give evening care. We would give the patient a partial bath, rub the patient's back, and straighten the bed and the room. Much later, when we studied medicines, again, we learned the importance of always putting things back exactly as we had found them.

We had to have uniforms before going into the hospital. Miss Viana Mcknown was the director of nursing education, and this was her first year here. Lots of changes were made when she came. First, the student nurses would no longer wear high-top black shoes with black stockings. Now we would wear white shoes with white stockings. Our dresses would continue to be blue chambray, but our aprons would be gored instead of gathered like those of the class ahead of us. We would not get our caps until January. All R.N.s worked twelve-hour days until 1941, when it was changed to eight-hour days.

We were given a ticket, and we went to Tapp's to be fitted for Vitality nursing shoes. These shoes had about a one-inch heel and were lace-up oxfords. We would be doing a lot of walking, bending, and stretching, so it was important that we were fitted properly. I was so excited to have my nursing shoes, the first step toward a uniform. It takes so little to make me happy sometimes.

Soon we had the rest of the uniform—the chambray dress with detachable collar and cuffs, and then the white gored apron with a white bib that crossed in the back. The class ahead of us wore the full uniform to and from the nurses' home, but we were to take off the apron and carry it back and forth so as not to take germs away from the hospital. However, the chambray dress did not look good without the apron, so we would try to get by like the older girls did. They gave us a hard time for a while, but later they gave it up.

With our basic knowledge, such as washing glasses, making beds, and so forth, and our uniforms, we were ready to go into the hospital to work. We started by giving evening care to patients. The patients were selected by someone in the hospital; they knew that we were new and were willing to take a chance. That's not exactly true; they were ready to get the little extras we could give them. I have to admit, I felt very important, even though I was somewhat afraid of doing something wrong. But we all did just fine. While we were giving evening care, we were also having classes each morning and early afternoon. Not a moment was wasted.

With the world situation as bad as it was and the possibility of the United States getting into the war, it was necessary to prepare as many nurses as possible and have them ready if needed. Of course, we had no idea of all that was taking place in our country. We did do "blackout" drills. In the older wings, we had a chart room with an outside window. These windows had been painted black so no light could be seen from the outside. Later, when the siren would sound, the nurses were to make sure all the lights were off except in the chart room.

If the weather turned colder during the night, the nurse was to secure blankets and make sure the patients were covered and warm. She was to close windows if it started to rain. Remember, at this time there was no air-conditioning, and since patients did not have early ambulation, everyone was in bed and had to be cared for regardless of the weather or other circumstances. It was a tremendous responsibility for young girls who were only eighteen years old. We matured rapidly.

At Textile, the bathrooms were located one on each floor. There were several stalls, and the light was on all night. One night, we had a tremendous thunderstorm, and I was heading to the bathroom. When I touched the doorknob to go in, there was sharp lightning and heavy thunder, and all the lights went out. I have to admit I was extremely frightened. Then, early in my nursing career, we had another storm exactly like the one at Textile. I was working nights alone with thirty-five patients. I shall never forget how I was shaking as I went into each room on the ward to make sure all the windows were closed and the patients were covered and comfortable. I can tell you, I grew up in a hurry!

When I first went into the hospital to work, somehow I was always in the old wing with the twelve-bed ward. Emptying bedpans wasn't so bad, but we had a number of women patients who dipped snuff. Many of the men chewed tobacco on the men's side, and, guess what, they had to spit frequently. They would spit into the emesis basin, and we had to empty it and rinse it out. I found that worse than bedpans. But after I did it over and over, it became just part of the job.

Soon we were assigned to a floor for a specific number of weeks. We would start working days, which was from 7:00 AM TO 3:00 PM, then afternoons from 3:00 PM to 11:00 PM, and finally nights from 11:00 PM to 7:00 AM. When we worked days, we would go onto the floors at 7:00 AM and leave just before 10:00 AM to get to our class. One time, I bathed ten patients between 7:00 AM and 10:00 AM. And you must remember that Miss Corley taught us that "cleanliness was next to godliness," and that all these patients were bedridden. There was not much time to be slack. We had to learn to move fast with everything we did.

A friend told me once that she was walking across campus at Clemson University when a man asked her, "Where did you finish nursing?" She answered, "How did you know I was a nurse?" and he answered, "I could tell by your walk." It became a habit, because we were always hurrying to or from something. My mother also had that brisk walk, and so do I. There were no intercoms when we came along. I don't remember seeing any overweight nurses back then, either. I might add that we were weighed each month to monitor our condition, I guess to see if we were running too much or too little. Now I know why a lot of women my age told me they wanted to be a nurse, but their parents would not let them because of the hard work involved. I told you earlier that I had been taught to have a strong work ethic, and I still have it. Really, it has served me well.

You're probably wondering if I ever had any social life with all the other things I've told you. Well, yes, I certainly did. In my high school years, I had one boyfriend. We both played basketball, but it was nothing like you see today. Each of us was #4 on our team; that's my lucky number. Remember, I was born on 4/4. When I went off to college, our relationship ended.

While I was at Textile, I had several boyfriends during the two years I was there. The first year, one guy who was older than I wanted me to quit school after my first year and marry him. He said, "You're sixteen years old; you know your own mind." I can't tell you how many times in my adult life I have remembered that and found it hard to believe. I had set my goal a long time ago. As I look back, I remember that most of the girls wanted to get married and have children. Frankly, I never did see myself being married with children.

In nursing school, we did have some free time. We had to be in our rooms from 7:00 PM until 9:00 PM each night to study, and the matron checked. We were free from 9:00 PM to 10:00 PM, which gave us time to go to the drugstore across the street for a Coke, ice cream, or whatever. The matron checked each day to make sure the nurses who had worked at night were in bed sleeping. We had a day off each week, but we still had to attend classes on that day if there were any.

Blanche Weldon, who was in my class, had a cousin who lived in Columbia, and she had a male friend she wanted Blanche to meet. So plans were made to go to a movie. He was bringing his friend, so Blanche encouraged me to go with them. I agreed and met my first husband, Earle Collum, that night, November 1, 1941. We went to the movie in Earle's new red Chevrolet sedan. He was working at Mutual Life Insurance Co. of New York.

Earle was a very nice-looking young man, and he had nice clothes as well as a new car. These things have always been important to young people. We enjoyed talking to each other, although there wasn't much time to talk since we had to get back in by 10:00 PM. The first night, he asked if he could call me sometime, and I told him he could. We dated for over three years before we married, but there's a lot to the story before that took place.

I had December 5, 6 and 7 off, so my daddy picked me up from the nurses' home, and we drove to our home in the country. I had a nice weekend, and he brought me back on Sunday afternoon at about five o'clock. When I walked into the nurses' home, everyone seemed upset, but no one said a word; it was a very strange feeling. In fact, it's hard to describe. Then I was told that the Japanese had bombed Pearl Harbor in Hawaii. They told me what they knew, and of course I was distressed as well. It was puzzling; we were so familiar with the war in Europe, but no one had ever mentioned

Asia. Later, we learned that some U.S. diplomats had been talking to their counterparts in Japan in recent weeks.

On Monday, December 8, everyone gathered around the radio in the parlor to listen to President Franklin D. Roosevelt declare war on Japan. We knew immediately that this would make a lot of changes in many ways since we were familiar with the blitz over London. We had learned about blackouts, and the windows in the chart rooms in the old wings had been painted with black paint quite some time ago. Other preparations had been made as well. But still no one had ever thought anything about Japan.

When an event of this magnitude occurs, it takes awhile for people to get over the shock. Almost immediately, young men and women were very angry and ready to go to war to fight to preserve our country. The Selective Service Act, known as the draft, was passed in 1940, and all eighteen-year-olds were required to register. Those chosen to serve were chosen by lottery. Knowing that this piece of legislation would send thousands of men and women to war, various installations had already been reactivated. The old Camp Jackson in Columbia became Fort Jackson in 1939. Columbia Army Air Base was built, as well as Shaw Field, in Sumter, South Carolina. The Charleston Navy Yard was going full tilt; in 1941, it launched twelve destroyers. The Lend Lease Act was also passed in 1941.

Fort Jackson was the site of basic training for all those enlisted or drafted for the infantry of the army. Thousands of men were there during the war and for a long time after. In fact, Fort Jackson is still going strong. It didn't take long for all these soldiers to find the nurses' home, with lots of beautiful single girls. Since the nurses worked rotating shifts, some were always available at any hour. Our parlor stayed full, someone played the piano, and there was lots of singing. Most of these men came from New York, New Jersey, Rhode Island, Massachusetts, and other states in the North. They were very loud and very unlike the men I was used to. The different cultures were frightening to me.

I read recently that South Carolina, in the early years of our country, had fewer immigrants than any other state in the union. There were two main reasons for this. We had no manufacturing, which attracted immigrants, and our weather was so hot and miserable in the summer. The cultures I've mentioned came mostly from much colder climates. After air-conditioning came to the South, the Northerners loved the South.

I never spent much time with these guys, but most of the other nurses felt differently about them. They dated them frequently, and some of them married. My best friend married one of these guys and learned later that he was a felon. She got a divorce at once. The other reason was, as I have said before, all the girls wanted to get married, which, as you know, was not my priority.

One girl went out with the best-looking guy of the bunch, and everyone was envious. But in a very short while she came flying back into the nurses' home. When asked about it, she said, "He had my garter belt unhooked by the time we reached the first signal light." There was no way I would ever go out with someone I did not know. In my family, it was always a joke that my daddy would have to know, "What does his daddy do?" Family was that important.

People did not go out to eat much during this time; it was too expensive. The women did not work and stayed home to prepare meals for the family. There were no restaurants on every corner, either. I know it sounds strange to the young people today, but one of the customs in Columbia was to park on Main Street and watch the people walk by. What was more interesting was that the stores were not open on Sunday, and that's when people really liked to watch. Earle and I did the same thing. We would just sit in the car and talk. It was definitely a safe date!

Soon it was January. After going in and out of the hospital to work for several months, we were pretty relaxed about working with patients. In January we received our caps. A senior nurse was chosen to "cap" a freshman nurse. I don't know how these seniors were chosen, but Manning Asman capped me. It was a meaningful ceremony, and we felt like now we were real nurses. We would wear the plain white cap until our senior year; then we would be awarded a black band to put on the cap to denote that we were seniors. The cap was an important part of the uniform. Each nursing school in the country had a cap that was especially designed for that school. One girl from Columbia went to work in California after her graduation and saw a nurse in a Columbia Hospital cap walking down the hall. She said it was so thrilling to find someone from home. Since we were at war, people were moving from place to place, so it was possible to find a cap from "home" almost anywhere. Nurses do not wear the cap much anymore. I have heard all kinds of reasons for this, but I still think it is part of the uniform. There are so many levels of staff providing nursing care in hospitals, and it is comforting to a patient if the person caring for him or her in a health facility is a "real" nurse. Much of our identity has been lost, and it makes me sad.

I told you earlier about the building of the hospital's east wing. All of the important people in Columbia had rooms on the first floor of the east wing when they were hospitalized. What is amazing to remember is that if someone just wanted to rest for a week or so, that person could check into the hospital for whatever time he or she needed to be up and running again. The rooms were about $5.00 a day. Can you believe it?

I was working on First East when I received my cap. There was an older man named Mr. Tool who had been in the hospital for a very long time. I suspect he had had a stroke, because he yelled a lot of the time but never really knew what was going on. It was my job to feed him his supper every night. He would open his mouth very wide, and I would put the food in. I stood between the light and the wall, and the shadow of my cap was cast upon the wall. I would bob my head up and down to watch the shadow. I was so proud of my cap.

The floors of the east wing had lovely solariums for patients and visitors. Several times, Earle came to sit in the solarium and watch me work. I was mostly flitting in and out of rooms. Once we had a young Columbia police officer in the first room by the chart desk. He told me it was worth being in the hospital just to watch my legs going to and fro.

In the early forties, when my rotation took me to the diet kitchen, I learned that the students actually prepared the food for the special diets. The big kitchen at Textile was totally different. My children always teased me about cooking institutional food: no salt, no sugar, and no fat! I remind them that that is the diet recommended for everyone now.

Next I was assigned to the operating room, which was too restrictive for me. After I had scrubbed and gowned, I could not touch anything that wasn't sterile, and I was very uncomfortable working there. The nurse anesthetist always kidded the doctor when any freshman nurse was in the OR for the first time. She would say, "Fresh meat, Charlie!" That didn't help, either.

When surgery was performed, the patient was asleep and completely covered except for the area that had been prepared for the surgery. Sometimes the surgeon went "digging" around, and it appeared to me like a horror movie.

When I scrubbed for an orthopedic surgery for the first time, the instruments were brought to the back table where I was, and I saw a hammer, chisel, saw, and all kinds of odd-looking instruments like one sees in construction work. That was a bit unnerving. One group of orthopedic surgeons behaved like clowns when they were using these instruments. It was upsetting to me. Since I was already timid about the whole thing, I asked my supervisor not to assign me to work with them again, and she never did.

In one case, the surgeon was doing an abdominal surgery, and I was to hold a retractor in place. This instrument held the skin and muscles out of the way so he could work in the small area. I was instructed not to take my eyes off the surgical site, because if you moved your eyes, you would automatically move the retractor. Surgeons didn't like that. On one occasion, we had a very long surgery, and I had been standing in one place holding a retractor for over three hours when the surgeon shouted, "Kick a chair under Wheeler—she's going down!" I didn't faint, but I was relieved by another nurse.

During my senior year, I was working on Isolation. We had a number of spinal meningitis cases in Columbia, so we had several patients on that ward. One boy, who was about twelve years old, kept climbing over the bedrails. I knew if he fell I would be held responsible. I called the intern on duty, and he came at once to help me.

We had about six interns each year who came to the Columbia Hospital to further their training. In the early forties, nurses could not take blood pressure or start an I.V. These interns became our friends, because they were always there to help us. Several nurses married young men who interned while I was there.

When I was in nursing, I was learning every day; student nurses did everything. There were no aides, no social workers, no health educators and none of the ancillary workers we have today. When I look back on it, it was amazing what we did learn. Not everything came from books.

I remember one particular incident when I was working in the emergency room alone. A man came running into the door screaming, "I have a little boy here who ran into the side of a moving car, and it almost tore his ear off!" I immediately started to run out to see about the situation. Then I stopped for a second to think about what I was doing, and what I *should* be doing. Then I grabbed a stretcher to take to the car to get the patient.

Many years later, when I was teaching first aid, I used this example to teach the students the necessity of "thinking" first. What should I be doing? I have never forgotten how much I learned in a few seconds that Easter Sunday.

The war was in full swing about the time I received my cap. Everywhere you looked were men and women in uniform. We had blackout drills, and a new course was added to our curriculum to give some necessary information on first aid and caring for large numbers of people, should this become necessary. There were women in WACS in the army and WAVES in the navy, but in the Marines they were called Marines. This was something new for our country. Before the war, most married women did not work outside the home. In fact, most men did not want their wives to work, because the husband was supposed to be the breadwinner for the family. A woman working was thought to make the husband look like he was not fulfilling his responsibility. Everything changed during the war, and much of it never returned to the earlier customs. My mother never did work outside the home, except for the one summer she relieved another nurse. But during the war, she taught home nursing to women in the country. Nearly all families had a Victory Garden, where they grew vegetables for home use. There were canneries, so the abundance of vegetables could be canned for later use. Gasoline was rationed, as were sugar, coffee, bacon, steak, and shoes. There were no silk stockings to be found. Since I was in training at the hospital, I was not involved in rationing. Of course, we were provided food and our uniforms, including the cap.

Everything in the United States was part of the war effort. War bonds were sold to raise more money, and schoolchildren bought war stamps to contribute to the effort. The country was united as never before to win the war. By this time, we were fighting on two fronts. We had the European theater and the Pacific theater. One of our favorite interns was taken into the service and sent to the Pacific theater, but he was killed before he reached his place of assignment. It saddened us all. Everyone was hungry for news and kept a close watch on how the war progressed.

Every nurse knew what divisions were at Fort Jackson and where many of the soldiers had gone. Mail was extremely important. We nurses did our part in trying to keep up the morale of those serving in the military. During the war, we had V-Mail, which was written on a special paper that was as thin as tissue paper and easier to handle in large volumes. I wrote to one of my high school teachers, a first cousin, and to some other guys who had no families. Everyone did the same thing. It was a concentrated effort to keep up morale.

The beautiful terminal building at Columbia Metropolitan Airport is part of the old Columbia Army Air Base (CAAB), which was built for World War II. We nurses all knew the different kinds of aircraft, and many civilians knew as well. At the CAAB, the pilots flew B25s. At the beginning of the war, there was no separate flying entity; it was part of the army known as the Army Air Corps. That all changed when the U.S. Air Force was established.

Earle and I were still seeing each other, and he knew that very soon he would be drafted. His parents had divorced when he was an infant, and he'd been reared by his grandparents in Perry, South

Carolina. At that particular time, there was quite a stigma attached to divorce. His mother, Lurline, went to work at Postal Telegraph in Columbia when Earle was about two years old. She would ride the train to Perry to see Earle on the weekends when he was growing up. He was seven years old before he saw his father. His father, Birdie D. Collum, was a conductor on the Southern Railroad but also owned a filling station and even sold some real estate on the side. There was always disagreement. She chided him for not doing more for Earle, and he thought she was harassing him all the time, which it appears she was. After this, Earle just gave up on going to college.

Earle told me that when he was growing up, the children at school always teased him by telling him he did not have a father. When he was in high school, he and his cousins went to Salley High School and played basketball. One day after basketball practice, when they were driving back to Perry, a car coming from the other direction hit them head on; it was a terrible crash. Earle's first cousin William, who was like a brother to him, was killed in the accident. Some others were killed, too. This was a very traumatic experience for Earle. On the way to the hospital, he held William's head in his lap. I have thought many times that he never fully recovered from that loss. Our youngest son is named William in memory of his cousin.

Only a few months after I met Earle, he started talking about us getting married. It seemed that this was exactly like my experience in college. I could not understand why getting married seemed to be the only thing young men and women were interested in. I suppose it was due to the way people had lived up until that time. There were few opportunities for women. If your family had money, you were able to attend college; if not, nursing seemed to be the next best thing. Beyond that was the telephone company or clerking in a store. There were some secretaries but not very many at that time, because that required extra schooling; many who could not afford the other opportunities could not afford business training.

Quite awhile ago, I was talking to a pilot I knew and just made the comment that I always wanted to be a fighter pilot. He asked, "Why didn't you?" It was very difficult to tell him that women, when

I was growing up in South Carolina, did not have the option of getting that kind of training; there was so little money. Remember it only cost my father $14.00 a month for me to go to college, because I worked in the kitchen for two years. When I went into nursing, we received a stipend of seven dollars a month for personal items; student nurses did all the work in the hospital.

Earle had a doctor friend who traded at his father's filling station. He wanted me to quit training and go to work in a doctor's office. I sort of ignored the suggestion, but he asked the doctor if he would talk to me, and he agreed. To please Earle, I did go to see that doctor. After I told him what Earle had in mind, he said, "Suppose you came to work for me and I fell in love with you. What then?" I don't think I answered, but he could see that really wasn't anything I was interested in. So he added, "I think you better stay where you are and finish your training." God has always been very close to me, and I knew he was there by the answer I received without having to say a word.

I thought that would end the pressure to get married, but I was wrong. Earle continually talked about it, urging me to give up nursing school. Finally, I asked why he didn't go see my mother and ask her opinion of me giving up nursing to get married. Of course, I knew what her answer would be, but he continued to press me. He went to see my mother, and she said she would absolutely not consent to me getting married. I don't think he ever liked my mother much after that.

In October of 1942, the draft was reaching many men as the war went on. Earle decided that he would enlist. If a man of draft age enlisted on his own, he could choose the branch of service where he would like to serve. Earle chose the Air Corps. This still was not the air force; that came later. He said he wanted to be a pilot. He was sent to Keesler Field in Biloxi, Mississippi, for his basic training. While the men were there, they took all kinds of tests to determine where best they could serve. After all was said and done, he did not qualify to be a pilot. He could have been a glider pilot, which he promptly rejected. Finally he was to be an airplane mechanic. He stayed there for three months while he was trained and was then sent to Shaw Air Field in Sumter, South Carolina. Later it became Shaw Air Force Base. His job there was working on the small trainer planes, until much later when the P-51 Mustangs were stationed at Shaw.

At about this time, the Cadet Nurse Corps was established. It was a means to entice young women to go into nursing and subsequently into the military. They were paid more and had snappy uniforms to wear when not working in the hospital. I was almost a senior nurse at this time, but we had the option of joining the Cadet Corps anyway. The nurses received their books free; before this, we rented our books. Earle begged me not to join the Corps; he did not want me to go into the military, even though we were told we did not have to enlist. He said, "I know if you ever leave Columbia, you will never want to come back." And he was probably right. I did not join the Corps, but I did want my books, but my father refused to buy them for me. He said I'd be finished training soon, so I'd be finished with the books. The idea that I might want them for reference when I started work would have been lost on him, so I just let it go. I did so want them, though.

The war was at its peak about this time. Islands in the Pacific became very familiar to us, because so many men were killed while taking them from the Japanese and struggling to hold them. European names were easier to understand than those of the islands. All the large manufacturing companies were involved in making war goods of whatever kinds were needed. No automobiles were made during the war; the last few were made in 1942. Many have speculated as to whether our country could ever mobilize to the extent it did during that period. We are such a diverse population now, unlike in the forties. I hope we never have to find out.

One of the last courses I took my senior year was a course about mental illness. Members of the class went to the South Carolina State Hospital For the Insane each week for the class. Earle was in town when we went one Saturday, and he picked me up. He said he had a surprise for me. He had gotten a marriage license for us. That was not exciting to me, but we didn't have to use it. He said, "I am going to carry it around over the sun visor in the car, because if you ever say you will marry me, I'll have to have it right then." I told him he was probably right.

There were many instances when a rumor went around that Earle's outfit would be going overseas. He would come to Columbia to tell me goodbye. All the nurses would say goodbye over and over to this one and that one. Earle never had to go, but there were so many who did and so many who never came back. All the guys just waited for the time when the war would be over and they could come home. They dreamed of all the things they wanted to do after the war, and Earle was no different. When men left their jobs to serve in the war, their jobs were there when they returned. Earle wanted to do something besides stay with the insurance company he had left behind. We spent a lot of time talking about all these things. I told him, "If I should marry you, I wouldn't want to have to support our family, but don't you one time ever tell me I can't work!" I had two special friends whose husbands would not let them work outside the home. He said, "I can promise you that."

Several times while I was in training, Miss McKown, Director of Nursing Education, called me to her office. She told me I was a good nurse and doing well, but, as smart as I was, she did not understand why I did not have straight A's on my subjects. I knew the material, and I knew how to use it, but making A's never did interest me. As you are reading this, I'm sure you can understand why I wasn't interested in grades. There were just too many other things going on.

You might be wondering if Earle and I were in love. I don't think either one of us even knew the meaning of the word. Earle told me all about his problems and said if I married him he wouldn't have these problems. He said also that he could succeed at anything if he had me for a wife. Could I really do that for him? I'm sure you know that one person cannot "make" another person; that is something a person has to do for himself. But at a young age, and lacking experience with situations like this, I believed that he might be right. He was at the nurses' home so much that all the students knew him and liked him. He did not hesitate to drive them someplace to dance if that was the request, and often it was.

I thought of the vow I had made at seventeen years of age: to spend my life trying to make things better for others. I prayed so many times for guidance in making a decision. Every obstacle I had put into the relationship seemed to fail. Was I supposed to "try to make his life better"? What about my life? I never had any answers. We had been going together for three years. Surely I should have made up my mind in that length of time, but I had never looked beyond my graduation due to the war and uncertainty about the future.

Our graduation was scheduled for May 25, after we had finished all our class work, but we would have to remain in school until we had finished three calendar years of training. Nurses were badly needed for the military, so even the state boards we had to take to receive the designation of registered nurse were scheduled to be given early after we had finished all of the class work.

On Sunday, June 4, 1944, Earle picked me up when I returned from the hospital. We drove to Main Street to park and watch the people go by. We saw lots and lots of soldiers, because there were several places for them to go for fellowship. A number of churches had such programs. While we were there, Earle started on the "let's get married" theme, as he had for almost three years now.

I said, "I'll tell you what. I will marry you tonight; but if we can't work it out, then we will forget the whole thing." He agreed. I never thought it could possibly happen, but he was sure it would. He called until he found a Lutheran pastor who agreed to marry us at his apartment that night. Then he called my roommate, Blanche Weldon, who was thrilled; she got an older nurse, Jo Frieda Huggins, from our class to come with her. We picked them up and went to the apartment, where the pastor met us. I shall never forget, he had two small children, and there was a playpen in the living room. He talked to us for awhile, and when he learned that Columbia was our home, he hesitated. The girls then told him about the license we'd had in the car for the last six months. So he performed the ceremony.

Blanche and Jo Frieda were thrilled to death, and I think I was just stunned! I never dreamed that he could pull it off. But at least now he would quit harping on getting married. We had to hurry to get back into the nurses' home before 10:00 PM. The big thing was that this had to be kept secret; we were not supposed to get married during our training. There were many who thought we were already married anyway.

For the next two days, June 5 and 6, we were at the capitol building taking our state boards. I did not learn until much later that I made the second-highest grade in my class.

The building that had been the black hospital had at this point been remodeled and converted into another wing of the white hospital. The third floor was designated an orthopedic floor, and I was put in charge of that floor. The war was still going on, and the student nurses were still running the hospital, with the exception of the supervisors, and there were very few of those.

# Marriage and Building a Family
## 1944-1958

Up until this time, I had not looked to the future at all. I was working very hard and looking forward to completing the three calendar years that were required for a diploma. But now that I had gotten married, although it was a strange sort of marriage, it was necessary that I look at the soon-to-be-different situation. Earle was very pleased with himself, since he had finally overcome all the stumbling blocks I had put forth. He wanted me to come to Sumter to live when I finished my training. He was still stationed at Shaw Field. I don't think I had really thought much about the change in my life, but I knew I would handle it well, like I did everything. Of course, I prayed a lot about it; as usual, God gave me the reassurance I needed.

Just before September 11, Earle found us a place to live. It was in a beautiful old white two-story house just off Main Street. We would have a large bedroom and a bath. Other parts of the house were rented also. Sumter was not a large town, so the airmen from Shaw kept everything pretty well filled up. I would continue to work in Sumter until the war was over.

The morning of September 11, 1944, was beautiful and sunny. Perhaps that was a positive omen. We loaded up my few possessions and headed for Sumter.

Sumter had just one small hospital, so I visited Tuomy Hospital and talked to the director of nursing. She told me that since they had a nursing school they did not need any help at all. However, they did keep a registry for private duty nursing demands, and she said I might be able to find some work there; but she did not think much work would be available. However, she did have a case right now if I could start tomorrow, and I assured her I could. After receiving directions and other information, I left the hospital feeling pretty good about the fact that at least I had a start.

The next morning, just before 7:00 AM, I reported for work at a lovely little white cottage and was greeted by a very friendly woman who expressed her appreciation that she now had some help with her husband, who had had a stroke and was comatose. I could tell she was tired and that this had been very difficult for her. I had not worked in a home before, but it was no problem; everything I needed was provided.

When I went to work on the third day, I was told that my patient was in poor condition. The doctor had told the patient's wife he had only a few more hours to live. At about 11:00 AM, he died. I did all the things that a nurse does when a patient dies, and I felt bad that I had not had the opportunity to get to know this lovely couple.

I called the hospital to report the patient's death. The director suggested that I come to the obstetric floor at the hospital to care for a distressed infant. The mother had delivered a twelve-pound baby, and, after a very difficult delivery, the baby was in poor condition. She suggested that I come to the hospital and care for the baby until my shift was over at 3:00 PM and charge each patient one half of the daily rate.

The baby was in very poor condition, but I did what she asked. At about 1:00 PM, the baby died. This did not make me feel good as a new graduate nurse. Having two patients die on the same day before 3:00 PM made me feel like maybe I wasn't supposed to be a nurse at all. Of course, I reasoned I had nothing to do with it; both of the patients had been near death when I first saw them. But to lose your first two patients on the same day, well, that wasn't what one looked for!

I guess you know that since we lived in one rented room it was necessary for us to eat out all the time, and if I couldn't work, where would the money come from? Days went by with nothing from the hospital, and we had no money. Earle's mother, who made very little at her job, gave us some money to help for a short while. But soon it became very clear to me that God did not want me in Sumter. We stayed in Sumter about two months, I think, but in that time I gained about twelve pounds from eating greasy food all the time and not exercising by running up and down halls.

At the end of the month, I knew I would have to go back to Columbia to find work. I went to the Columbia Hospital and saw Dr. Weston, Jr., who was an outstanding pediatrician. He asked me to come by his office the next day if I had time. I had lots of time. He'd known me well as a student, but I had no idea why he wanted me to come to his office.

When I arrived in the waiting room, it was filled with children of all ages, with lots of crying. You wouldn't believe how timid I was. I just took a chair and did not speak to anyone. In the hospital we were taught not to ever interrupt a doctor, and it was obvious, even to me, that he was very busy. He shared office space with his father, who was also a pediatrician. When most of the patients had been seen, Dr. Weston, Jr., came to the waiting room looking for me. He asked why I hadn't let the receptionist tell him I was there. He wanted to offer me a job working for him. I accepted right away, and he wanted me to start the next day. I knew then that God was looking out for me.

I immediately started looking for a place for Earle and me to live. Everything was full of military families, even small apartments. I looked and looked and finally found a one-bedroom with a small kitchen and a bath that would be shared with another couple. Both apartments were upstairs in College Place, a suburb of Columbia. I would have to ride the bus to and from work, and I would have to walk about three blocks to the bus line. It wasn't great, but it was the best I could find.

I found myself a bit lonely since I had been in the nurses' home the last three years, but Earle was able to come to Columbia often. I often wondered how he could get the gas since it was rationed, but he said he had a way, so I let it go.

Dr. Weston's office was a bit cramped and had an oil-circulating heater that did not heat the place much at all. Many of the mothers did not want us to undress their babies in the cold room, but Dr. Weston assured them it was all right. Off his office was an enclosed porch where we saw the black children. Dr. Weston never charged poor people, and later he always saw all my children and never charged me anything. It's an amazing contrast to the practice of the physicians of today.

\*\*\*

In the spring of 1945, I thought I was pregnant and made an appointment with Dr. Talbert, a general practitioner, and he confirmed my suspicions. Our baby would be due about the middle of October. I remember so well walking from the bus stop with this great secret deep within my heart. Somehow I felt different when I considered that I would become a mother. All the yellow flowers, my favorites, were in bloom at this time, and I don't remember ever seeing them quite as beautiful. To this day, when these yellow flowers are in bloom, it makes me feel happy!

I continued to work for Dr. Weston, Jr., until the last of May, when he hired my childhood friend Ella Ruth Fleming. She had finished Columbia Hospital Nursing School the year before I did. I bought a folding lawn chair, we called them, and teased everyone at the office by saying, "I'm going to the country, and I plan to sit in this chair and wait for my baby to come!"

In July of 1945, Earle's mother, Lurline, remarried M/Sgt. Curtis L. Ingram. He was stationed at Fort Jackson and had been in the military for over twenty years. Ingram was reassigned to Fort Belvoir, Virginia, near Washington, D.C. Lurline always said she would not marry again until she saw Earle happily married, so then things sort of fell into place.

Earle's mother Lurline had been living in an apartment on Assembly Street in Columbia. There were three apartments in a large house: one upstairs, one across the hall, and the one she lived in, which was the smallest. There were two large rooms with twelve-foot ceilings, a tiny kitchen, and a small bathroom, which had been added on some years later. She paid $15.00 a month for the apartment. Lurline made arrangements for Earle and me to take over her apartment when her husband Ingram was transferred to Fort Belvoir, Virginia.

Somehow we bought a cedar chest, a bedroom suite, and an electric refrigerator. Lurline left a couch, dining table and four chairs, and a buffet. The kitchen stove had two gas burners that worked and two that did not. In the corner was a gas water heater that had to be lit, each time you wanted hot water from the tap, and a small cabinet for dishes.

We lived in this little apartment for three winters. The first winter, we had an upright coal heater that had to be started each morning. The second year, we bought an Ashley wood-burning heater. This helped some, because the fire could be banked at night, and the apartment did not get quite as cold. The last year, we bought an oil-circulating heater. Finally we had some heat at night.

In May, before Lurline moved, I stayed with her, and there were several days in May when she would build a fire in the coal heater so we could be warm. Houses with twelve-foot ceilings were built to be cool in the Southern summer heat. I guess since our summers are long, no one was too concerned about the winters.

# Emily Kathryn Collum
## August 30, 1945

Earle was home the last weekend in August, so we went to my family home in the country for the weekend. The sunset on August 29 was a vibrant red and gold. I remember commenting to Earle how beautiful it was. After supper, we went to bed for the night. About 2:00 AM my water broke, and I went into labor about six weeks early. We hurriedly loaded our car and headed twenty miles to the Columbia Hospital. Since the delivery was early, they would not give me anything except a Nembutal for the pain. My first baby, a beautiful little seventeen-inch-long baby girl, was delivered. She weighed six pounds three ounces. Her name had already been chosen. She would be Emily Kathryn, and we would call her Kay, which was popular at that time. But when I had her in my room the first time, and after I had done the "monkey check" for fingers and toes, I looked at her and said, "You are my Katy!"

I had reserved a private room in the obstetrics ward, which was the second floor of the east wing. At that time, patients stayed about a week after delivery. Earle had to go back to Shaw Field. My mother drove in from the country just once, and Lurline neither drove nor had a car. So instead of having lots of people around to share my joy in having a beautiful, healthy little girl, I was alone in the room except when Katy was brought out for me to nurse her.

Now seems to be the best time for me to tell you I had never been around a baby except when I worked in the nursery and in pediatrics. In the nursery, the babies were in their bassinets all the time, and changing diapers was easy because they weren't going anywhere. Those in pediatrics were sick, so the situation was about the same. I told my friends later that I kept waiting for the nurse who would work the next shift to arrive and care for the baby; but sorry, when you have your first baby, no matter how much you need help, sometimes there isn't anyone to do it, and you just muddle through the best you can. So that's what I did.

Even after we had five children, Earle said I never did learn how to put on a diaper that would not fall down. After each child started walking, most times the diaper would end up around the baby's ankles; sometimes it would trip them, and down they would fall. I can tell you right now that handling diapers was not my calling! About diapers: everyone was using cloth diapers when my children were born. This meant washing diapers every single day for about two-plus years per child.

When my first two children, Katy and Ann, were born, we were still living in the little apartment. I would light the gas water heater and put the diapers in the bathtub. I knelt on my knees, and, using a small scrub board, I scrubbed and rinsed them twice. They looked very clean. Then I would take them to the back porch, where some lines had been strung between the posts, and with clothespins, I would hang them up. Now that seemed to be okay, but wait. Behind our big house was the Jefferson Hotel, and they had a coal furnace with black smoke pouring out all day and night during the winter. My lovely washed diapers had flecks of coal dust on them the whole time we lived there.

Earle and I had an experience that we have never forgotten and still talk about to this day. Our first winter in the apartment, with our little baby several months old, we had the coal stove. Katy did not wake up for her bottle like usual, but I woke up, and the room was very cold. I went to the crib and reached for the baby, and she was ice cold. I became very distressed, and I frantically called Earle. He got right up and came over to the crib. When he touched her, she started crying. Then we knew she was all right. But never will we ever forget the fears we had at that instant when our little Katy was stone cold.

World War II ended in Europe in May of 1945, and Japan surrendered on August 15, 1945. The war was finally over, and it was time to start rebuilding our lives into some sort of normal. There were celebrations everywhere; it had been a long, sad episode in our country's history. Now was the time to make decisions about the future. Many who had left jobs to serve returned to those jobs. A very large number took advantage of the GI Bill and headed to institutions of higher learning to complete their education. Earle was discharged as a corporal in November 1945, unsure about what he wanted to do; but he had a specified time to decide.

Earle ruled out the GI Bill and college early on. I believe it was because of the constant disagreement between his divorced parents. Then he decided he would like to have a service station since his dad had done well with the one he owned. To learn more about it, he decided to go to work at a station to see if that was the right thing. He had a friend who had a station, and he went to work for him. He would come home all greasy, dirty, and smelling like gasoline and oil. It wasn't long before he knew that wasn't for him. I never said anything, but I sure was glad he changed his mind about that opportunity.

Then Earle decided he would sell life insurance fulltime. That didn't work out, either. That kind of job requires a lot of self-discipline, and he just could not seem to get the hang of it. Then he went to an employment agency to see if they had anything he could do. The agency called back in a few days and said the only thing they had was driving a milk truck.

After this experience, he decided to go back to the Mutual Life Insurance Company and do premium accounting, which was the job he'd left when he went into the service. It became clear that we would have to have more income to survive.

Ella Ruth Fleming, my childhood friend, had married one of those soldiers I was so afraid of. Later she found that he was wanted by the police in his home state, so she had to get out of the marriage. South Carolina had very strict laws regarding divorce, but in this case it could be achieved, though it would take quite a while. Her mother and father would not let her come home to stay, so she decided to come live with us. We had only one large closet, but we put a rollaway bed in it, and every night Ella would roll it out and put it back the next morning. She agreed to pay us $40 each month and meals when she was there. She was still working for Dr. Weston, Jr. having taken my job before Katy was born.

Well, what can I say to all this? I had a new husband, a new baby, and a boarder; and remember, I didn't know how to cook or care for an infant. It was at this point I realized that my marriage was not a dream but a nightmare. I missed my work and the other nurses. I knew even then that things were not going to be easy for us. When Ella came home from work, she sat on the couch and never offered to help me, even by setting the table. But there's more. Her aunt and her husband would come over almost every night just to sit and talk. I don't know if you can see me in this picture or not, but it was horrible for me. Even now when I think about it, I remember how difficult it was for me and Earle. This went on for about a year, but I didn't complain; nothing could be done at this point.

When Ella Ruth's divorce was finalized and she moved out, I realized I was pregnant again. I hired a young black woman named Lily to work for us, and I registered to do private-duty nursing at night. I reasoned that Lily could care for Katy while I slept during the day, and I wouldn't be away from her. Earle was good with Katy, so he would care for her at night. There was only one problem: I am not a night person! That was the hardest money I've ever earned. If a night nurse can get her patient to sleep all night, that was the sign of a good nurse. However, most patients did not want a light burning in the room at night, and they didn't hesitate to expect you to sit in the dark and stay awake. I'll say it again: I am not a night person! I would go to Central Supply and get a light on a drop cord, and I would hook it to the springs under the bed. In this pitiful arrangement, I would sit in a straight chair, and if I bent over far enough, I could read by the light under the bed. That worked fairly well until my tummy prevented me from bending over far enough. I'll say again: I am not a night person!

# *Ann Elizabeth Collum*
## July 13, 1947

I always had enough warning when my baby was coming. July 13, 1947, was a hot Sunday. Earle left the house about noon to take Katy to my mother's to stay until the baby was born. After he left, one of my high school classmates called me to chat. He said, "I hear you have a little girl." I answered, "Yes, but soon I'll have another baby." He said, "When?" and I said, "Tonight." Was he ever shocked! Earle always said he drove very fast getting Katy to my mother's, and when he returned, I was nonchalantly talking on the phone. It was a funny day. Ann Elizabeth was born about 10:30 PM at Providence Hospital. She weighed seven pounds twelve ounces. Dr. Pope, an obstetrician I knew well from my student days, delivered her. Ann was only two weeks early.

We were still in the little apartment. Many old people were living around us, and each time I went out of the house I knew they were watching me. When Earle took me to the hospital to have Ann, he really laughed, because I wore church clothes and a hat. Hats were popular then. I did not want them to know where I was going. I never knew whether I fooled them or not.

During the winter of l947–48, we realized we needed to find us somewhere else to live. With two small children, the place was filling up fast. Housing was still going for a premium, so we looked and looked. Finally, we found a new yellow stucco house near Cayce. It wasn't large, but what a relief it was to have more room. Cayce is a suburb of Columbia, and it was pretty far out. However, there was a bus line nearby, so getting to work would not be a problem. The big thing for a person who had always lived in Columbia was the fact that anything west of the Congaree River was considered to be inferior. We knew that, but with very little money, it was the best we could do. We moved when Ann was eight months old.

Katy had a tricycle, so she had a place to ride, and Ann was crawling all around the house. One day, when I changed Ann's diaper, I was shocked to find eight screws about one inch long just lying in the diaper with the stool. It really frightened me, but there was no use being upset now; they had passed all the way through without causing any damage to her system. The house was very new, so we assumed that the screws had been left on a windowsill or on the floor and she'd just swallowed them. I do feel that the Lord was watching over us every day.

South Carolina is part of the Bible Belt, and practically everyone went to church each Sunday. If a new family moved into the area, the first question was, "Where do you go to church?" or "What denomination are you?" Consequently, since the area was primarily Christian, Easter was of tremendous importance. A large number of families received their salaries or hourly wages at the end of the week. So the Saturday before Easter, Main Street in Columbia was packed with black and white people buying dresses, hats, and shoes for the Easter Sunday services. This was good for us. Earle worked his office job for five days and then worked at Marilyn Shoe Store on Saturdays. He did that for many years, and it helped us stay afloat.

My mother and daddy continued to come to Columbia every Saturday to buy the things we did not grow in the country. They would bring us all kinds of vegetables and eggs and most times a fryer "on foot." It was my job to kill the chicken and dress it. It was a great help to us, and they were very glad to do it. During this period of time, I guess you could say I was a somewhat typical housewife.

Our next-door neighbors, who owned the rental house, told me their church was selling an old pump organ for $15.00 and asked if I would like to have it. I was happy to get it since I loved to play music so much. I was a stay-at-home mom, and it would help me enjoy my music again. So the neighbors and Earle went to Cayce and picked up the organ for me.

Earle's Aunt Fanny lived in the Camp Fornance section of Columbia, and she wanted us to live there near her. Soon a house across the street became vacant, and she contacted us. We went over to look at the house. It was on a corner lot and had very large rooms with very worn, bare floors and no cabinets at all. It was sort of a bare-bones house. But it would get us out of the Cayce area. My parents were not happy with us in Cayce, either. It's strange, but after living in a particular part of a town, moving to another area is like moving to another state.

This was not too far from where my parents had lived when I was growing up. After spending a year in Cayce, we moved back into Columbia. The little house in Cayce was brand new when we moved in, so trying to get this old house in presentable shape took quite a bit of effort. There was a central hall where we put our oil-circulating heater. Earle found a section of an old counter somebody somewhere had thrown away. It was pitiful, but we brought it in for the kitchen. It was not a place I was proud of, but both our families were glad to have us there.

While we were living in the old house, Earle's father had a heart attack. When he was discharged from the hospital, he came to stay with us for about a week. This gave me an opportunity to get to know him, and I was impressed. He seemed to be a very nice person, not at all like the man Lurline was constantly telling us about. He was pleased with his two grandchildren. He thought I was a very fine wife for Earle, but he said the only thing wrong was that Earle was too much like his mother. This became more evident as time passed.

Birdie, Earle's dad, could see that this house was not a place I should live with two small children. Later, he offered to buy the vacant lot behind the old house, which would make it possible for us to build a new house. The lot cost $400. We were very excited about it. I had been drawing house plans for years, yearning for a new house for our family. Homer Blackwell, who went to Textile with me, had taken the GI Bill and completed his education to become an architect. After the lot was bought, I got in touch with Homer, and he drew up the official plans from my drawings. The house was 1,200 square feet and cost $4,500. I remember signing the thirty-year mortgage and thinking how far in the future it would be before it would be paid for.

During this time, I went to work at Providence Hospital on a part-time basis. I had inquired at the Columbia Hospital, but they did not hire any part-time nurses. Providence was glad to get me. I worked from 7:00 to 11:00 PM so Earle could be home with the children. At one point, I worked Sunday only from 3:00 to 11:00. This worked well, because the regular nurse had every Sunday off, and I had a babysitter. All this for $1.00 per hour! I enjoyed my work at Providence. Sister Ursula, the director of nurses, liked me and was very kind to me, and we became good friends. Later, when I went back to private duty, she called me several times to care for one of the other nuns who needed a nurse.

By the time we moved into our new house, I was pregnant again. Sarah Jane was born on January 11, 1951. She was a beautiful baby and weighted six pounds twelve ounces. She was named for Earle's mother and his grandmother Smith. So things were looking up somewhat. I just loved the nice new house, and it had a special meaning since I had drawn the plans. We lived there for nine years. All the children learned to crawl down that hall.

# Sarah Jane Collum

## January 11, 1951

I delivered Sarah Jane at Providence Hospital. At this very time, Earle was offered a transfer to Shreveport, Louisiana. All the people from the office came to visit us, but no one asked about the baby or wanted to see her. All they could talk about was the transfer. Of course, at this point, that was not what I wanted to hear. They wanted to know how I felt about it. Earle and I had not had time to even think about it, much less talk about it.

About this time, office technology was coming onto the scene, and there would be many changes in how procedures would be done. We talked about Earle taking some courses to prepare himself for the coming changes, but he wasn't interested at all in keeping up. He decided he would not take the transfer, and he knew he would not be offered another opportunity. He said, "I will always be able to make a living in Columbia."

As usual, God was with us, and Earle did not have to tell the company he was not going to take the transfer. The man in Shreveport turned down his transfer, too. So things remained the same. With three small children, I stayed home for almost two years, but we had a difficult time; I was not able to work, and prices were escalating on everything. Earle's salary was very low, and I remember going to the store with our three girls and crying on the way home because I did not have enough money to get all the things I needed. The stress was beginning to take its toll on me. I started having problems with my stomach. My stomach is my signal, and when it acts up, I know I'm in trouble.

I made an appointment with Dr. Pope and went in to see him. He did a lot of tests and finally told me, "Wheeler, go to work! I have known you for years now, and you will never be happy if you aren't working." I had to admit he was probably right, but there wasn't any way I could go to work at that time.

✳✳✳

Our new house was just across the street from the elementary school, and Katy was just about ready to start school. She had been going to the preschool at Earlewood Park. She had a part in the little play and wore a cape, but instead of doing as she was directed, she just waltzed around, swinging the tail of her cape. I've already told you that I knew nothing about rearing children, and it upset me that she was not doing what she was supposed to do. Miss Barron, the director, just laughed at me and assured me that at five years old it was common for a child to do "his or her" own thing. When I was growing up, I was not allowed to make even one small mistake, so that was all I knew. I have told Katy many times that I wished I could rear her again. I made so many mistakes, and, as you read this, I will show you many times when I could have used some expert knowledge. However, after blundering through rearing five children, I haven't yet seen anyone who says they knew how to rear children before it became their responsibility. There are some exceptions; and it's those people who have never had children who seem to have all the answers. But they never have to live with their mistakes like I have.

I have one very special memory. When Katy was in the about the third grade, she brought a little girl home with her. At the door, I heard her say, "Come see my mother; she is a funny mother!" So she brought her back to the bedroom where I was sewing.

You are probably remembering that I did not know how to sew when I married. I would like to tell you how I learned. The companies that made chicken feed were still selling the feed in cloth bags. Mother was constantly making little sun dresses for Katy and Ann, the only two children I had at that time. The problem was she made them so big that they really did look like sacks, and I was embarrassed for them to wear them. I think by now you know how much my mother meant to me, and I wouldn't have hurt her feelings for anything. So the only course for me was to learn to sew myself. I went to Sears and bought a sewing machine for $10 down and $10 each month until it was paid for. Then I bought two patterns and studied them until I could sew pretty well myself.

I used to tell my friends that when I worked I had no time to sew, and when I stayed home I had no money to buy fabric! Later, when we lived in Houston, I was good enough to make all my square-dance dresses.

My father was finally able to retire in 1945, and he continued to work very hard, doing the things he liked so much like digging in his garden and growing things. He had a huge strawberry patch and grew asparagus and all the seasonal vegetables. Of course, he had his beloved chickens, as well as turkeys and guineas. It was an exciting place, and he was very happy. With my mother's wonderful cooking, using fresh milk and butter, my father had exactly what he wanted.

My mother still milked the cow twice a day. I have no idea how she learned to do that. I never did even try. But there was one exception. My mother was just as sharp as my father and just as stubborn, so there was a clashing of minds and voices on many occasions.

My mother's half-brother Alvin and his wife from California came to visit my parents. One day, Alvin called me and said, "Emily, your daddy has had a stroke, and your mother's face is paralyzed." This sounded a bit strange to me, but sure enough, that was what had happened.

I took Daddy to the hospital. After he was admitted, he had two more strokes. I learned later that he had passed out at two fires before he retired. I asked if his blood pressure was high, and he told me that the fire chief had called the doctor each time; when the doctor checked him, his blood pressure was normal. The supposition was that his blood pressure had spiked under the stress of the fires, and, of course, he had lost consciousness.

Mother's paralysis on the left side of her face is known as Bell's palsy. It has to do with the seventh cranial nerve in the brain. Lots of people have had Bell's palsy. Sometimes it clears up, and sometimes there are residual effects. Mother had trouble singing, which she loved to do, and it broke her heart. Her one vice was she liked to drink one Coke a day from the glass bottle. She could no longer do that. For quite some time she could not close her left eye, and when it became dry, it was very painful. It hurt me so much to watch her give up the little things she loved so much.

It was ironic, I guess, that Curtis Ingram, Earle's step-father, was discharged from the army about this same time, and he and Lurline moved back to Columbia from Fort Belvoir, Virginia. They bought a house in West Columbia, which was west of the Congaree River. Lurline was never happy there, because it was too far from where we lived. I think that was why Ingram wanted to stay there. But guess who won?

I started doing private duty again, but no more nights. I was working the 3:00 to 11:00 PM shift this time. I had three little girls, so I would get up and have breakfast with the family and then get Katy and Ann off to Fannie McCants Elementary School across the street. Then I would wash diapers, clean the house, and cook supper. When Earle came home, he would give the children their supper and put them to bed. Some nights, after I came home, I would sew for a couple of hours, but not too often.

Private-duty nursing is a very interesting job. It can be boring, busy, or a great experience. The patient is paying for your services, so it can be good or bad depending on the chemistry between the patient and the nurse. At this time, I was still a young nurse in many ways, and I have always credited this experience with teaching me patience. The nurse, according to my standards, should always be "up" and always be pleasant and pleased to be providing care to someone less fortunate at the time. So I did well doing private duty. Here are a few examples.

I had a female patient once who was seventy-two years old. She was from New Jersey and was a companion to an older woman. The two women were in Camden, South Carolina, visiting a wealthy family. It seems that Miss Peay fell on the sidewalk in front of the house and broke her hip. The gracious homeowner wanted to do everything he could to give her excellent care. Miss Peay had a nurse for each of the three shifts, and she thoroughly enjoyed the attention she received. She had received many potted plants. When I watered them, I put too much water on them, and it ran out all over the table and the floor. Did she give me a hard time? I'll say, and rightfully so. This experience taught me how to take care of potted plants. The other thing with Miss Peay was that she wanted me to read to her each afternoon. Of course, the books were very thick. It is a good thing I am an avid reader myself, because this went on the whole time I cared for her. You could make a long list of things I learned from this one patient.

Let me tell you about Mrs. Day. I was her only nurse, and I worked 7:00 AM until 3:00 PM. Mrs. Day had had surgery, and I was told that she was dying from cancer. I stayed with her for about three months. We took no days off when we were on private duty; we stayed until the patient no longer needed a nurse for whatever reason. She had a drainage tube from her abdomen, and it drained foul-smelling fluid. When Mrs. Day would get weak, she would be given a blood transfusion, and she would perk right up for quite a while. After being very close to her for a very long time, I thought she did not seem to fit the pattern of one dying with cancer. I had some special feelings about her condition and did not know how to try to help her. Her surgeon was a very young doctor who was new to the Columbia area, but she also had a urologist. The urologist had taught me as a student, and all the students loved him. I have already told you that we were taught that we should always stand in the presence of a doctor and never interrupt him. I prayed long and hard about this and decided I should speak out no matter what. I asked Dr. B. to meet me in the dining room, and I told him my suspicions about Mrs. Day. I told him that I felt a mistake had been made in her surgery, and I would like for the surgeon to go back in and see if he could rectify it. All the way home and for the next twenty-four hours, I did not know what would happen to me for my boldness. I prayed not only for Mrs. Day but for myself as well. The next thing I knew, Mrs. Day had been posted for surgery. The day of her surgery, I paced the floor; what if I had been wrong? Suppose she died? Suppose they took my license? But I knew that the Lord was with me, so I just kept praying. After surgery, the report showed that everything had been repaired, and she would recover. I had been right! Mrs. Day's daughter, who knew that I had insisted on surgery, told me later. "You'll remember this case as long as you live, won't you?" I have, and Mrs. Day told everyone, "Emily would not let me die!"

But there was another case where I didn't do as well. Mr. T. was in the hospital for gallbladder surgery, and I went on duty with him from 3:00 to 11:00 the day of the surgery. He was a lovely old white-haired man, and all three of his nurses loved him. When he had his eighty-fifth birthday, the day nurse and I bought him a cake, little hats, and things for a "party." He enjoyed it so much, and so did we. When I went to work two days later, I found that he had had a stroke and was in a coma. I was broken-hearted but tried not to show my feelings too much. When his surgeon came in later and saw him, he turned to me and said, "I want you to get him down to X ray for a skull film today." I looked at him and replied, "Do we have to?" Well, I guess I don't have to tell you that I was really told off in no uncertain terms. Later, another of his doctors came in and found me crying. He said to me, "Don't cry, Emily. He was trained at Johns Hopkins, and that's the way they are trained. I appreciate the fact that you were concerned about having the patient endure the pulling and tugging that would take place, since he is unconscious." I am so glad that nursing has come such a long way. No longer do nurses have to put up with this type of behavior.

Miss S. was a single nurse in her fifties, and I went on duty with her from 7:00 to 3:00 the day after Christmas. She had a malignant brain tumor. I stayed with her every day until Easter the next year. She lost consciousness the second day I was there, and there was great concern about getting fluids in her since she could not eat. But what was interesting about her was the fact she never had to have I.V.s. I'm sure you have seen little babies nurse and have seen how they can suck. This is an instinct, and Miss S. did that. I would touch her lip in a certain place, and she would start sucking away and could drink a whole glass of fluid at one time. Even the doctor could not believe it until I showed him how I could get her to take fluids.

I'll tell you about one more situation, one that was a bit different. The nurses' registry served any facility that needed private-duty nurses. The University of South Carolina had a flu outbreak, and the infirmary was filled with students. The only option was to open the penthouse of the Russell House, the student center, to house patients. I was called and worked from 3:00 to 11:00 there for several weeks. It was an interesting experience; the patients were all football players. I'm not a football fan, but they did have a good year that year.

You have read enough of this book to know how important nursing was to me. One Labor Day in the early fifties, Earle and I, with the three children, planned to go to the park for a picnic. But a phone call came, and it was the registry. It seems a woman had delivered a twelve-pound baby, and the baby was in acute distress. I was not registered at the time, but after trying everyone who was off, she called me to see if I would go take care of the baby.

I shall never forget walking out into the backyard with tears streaming down my face to tell Earle that I could not go to the park because I had to go to work. He understood, because he had gone through nursing school with me. In the forties, nurses were trained on the medical model, and our work was to come before anything else. Now it is not that way; it is an occupation, just like other jobs. Is that better? If you put it in the context of other changes in the healthcare system, it has to be this way.

What I have been writing about now took place in the 1950s. This is viewed as the peaceful, quiet time when Eisenhower was our president. We were not at war, and things had reverted to normalcy after the upheaval of World War II. But it was anything but peaceful and quiet for me.

Ann seemed to have something wrong with her skin. After taking her to the doctor, we learned that she had psoriasis. She has had this all her life. Sometimes it is really bad, and sometimes it is not. But for years and years I rubbed some sort of coal tar or greasy something or other on her every day. We found that when we went to the beach she always seemed to be better. So I ascertained that it was the saltwater. I tried putting salt in the tub, but it made no difference. We tried everything. Our dermatologist tried so hard to help her. My mother had psoriasis, and later Ann's son had it as well. We do know that it is inherited; fortunately, it skipped me.

In 1953, I was pregnant again. This time I wanted a boy. I felt like all men want a son, and I thought maybe Earle would see the need to get more education. He didn't. He wanted to sell life insurance on his own. Just like the first time, it didn't work out for him.

Later, he went to work for another insurance company; he stayed there maybe a year, and then he was let go. I kept encouraging him to think of what he would like to do and then take courses to prepare for some other kind of job. But he wasn't interested. I told him the way to keep a job is to prove yourself absolutely necessary to the company so they won't let you go. That didn't work, either.

Even though I was still working all the time, I was involved with our church. I sang in the choir for many years and taught Sunday school for the third grade for a number of years; I really did enjoy that. One year, at the beginning of Lent, I gave each child a gladiola bulb. On Easter morning, three of the children brought in their flowers, which had bloomed for Easter. I thought it was a great way to teach the concept of the Resurrection. Later, I taught the tenth grade, which was about other Christian denominations.

I kept comparing myself to Hannah in the Bible, who also wanted a son. I prayed to God all the time, and, like Hannah, I promised God that if I had a boy I would give him to the Lord. I was sick quite a bit with this pregnancy, but I kept going. Once we went to the beach with friends who had three boys, and we took our three girls, and the ocean waves did not help my stomach at all.

In November, I had a case at Providence Hospital, so I went to the office to make reservations for my baby's birth. The girl asked, "When is your baby due to arrive?" I answered, "The doctor says around April 15, but it will be in March." She said, "Are you having a C-section?" I said, "No, but he will be born on March 10." Earle Smith Collum, Jr., was born on March 10, 1954. God is with me!

# Earle Smith Collum, Jr.
## March 10, 1954

While I was in the hospital after Smitty was born, I told everyone that now I would have to have another baby. I did not want only one boy with three sisters. I laughed and said, "I think that would be a bit much for him!" He was called Smitty from day one.

From the day he was born, Earle's mother took him over as if he belonged to her. Smitty, my only boy, was so special to me, and I tried to bring about a change without upsetting anyone. But since I was working, I really couldn't do much.

My parents were still living in the country. My daddy had rehabilitated himself before it was in vogue. Mother had been told that he wouldn't get out of bed, but he did, and that he would never walk, but he did. He needed to use a cane? No way! But caring for everything they enjoyed was too much of a chore for my dad, and Mother worked very hard, but she, too, needed to have a smaller place.

Well, guess what? There was one lot across the street from us, next door to Earle's parents. I really was concerned about that, but since I was the only person who could look out for them, it would be easier for me if they were nearby. So Mother sketched out what she wanted in the way of a house, and Earle and I helped her get it built.

Later, if Smitty went over to see my parents, Earle's mother would run out into her front yard and wave a candy bar in the air and call him to come get the candy. Of course, as any child would do, he ran to her house. I felt very bad about it, but there was nothing I could do. Whenever our family had a problem, Earle was helpless.

My daddy was glad to be back in the city, because he had sidewalks and he walked several miles every day. Mother missed living in the country, and I had very little time to spend with her with work and a large family, but she went to church with us in a scheduled way. Our children sang in the choir. On Sundays, our routine was that Earle, my mother, and the children went to the early service while I started the dinner. Then I went to Sunday school and to later church and sang in the choir. I guess you could say we attended in shifts for many, many years. The church we attended was the same one I'd gone to as a small child. Mother really loved the church, but Daddy did not feel able to go, although he considered himself a very strong Lutheran.

Earle was still unsettled about what he wanted to do. What skills he had were not of much use since the newer technology was on the scene, and I urged him to think of what he would like to do and try to work toward it. He wasn't sure what he would do. When he did get a job, he would come home and tell me that he was doing all the work. The other people there didn't work hard at all. I believed this for a number of years. I never wanted to doubt that my husband was telling the truth, but later I knew he was the one not working. At this point, I knew I couldn't depend on Earle for our retirement. I began to wonder whom I could depend on. It would have to be me!

In the mid-fifties, the space program was just getting started, and rockets were being sent into space. Now, at this time, I became pregnant again. I remember going to a movie with my friend Dot Dula. The news being shown at the theater had a good close-up view of a rocket being sent into space. The power of it was actually frightening to me. I kept thinking of the coming changes and what it would be like for my fifth baby.

During the pregnancy, I was still doing private duty, now from 3:00 to 11:00. One patient's husband stayed in the room with me, as many husbands did. There was no relief for supper since there were not many nurses available to handle the needs of the patients on the floor. I took peanut butter on cheese crackers with me and bought a carton of chocolate milk. That's what I wanted. Her husband couldn't get over me eating that every night. Of course, he did not know I was pregnant.

# William Wheeler Collum
## June 12, 1958

My second little boy, William Wheeler, was born on June 12, 1958. His weight didn't do as well as the doctor expected, but I assured him, "Just let me take him home, and he will be fine."

After having several children, when you have another one, you take him home, put him on the floor, and very soon he is running with the others. I was back at the Columbia Hospital for William's birth. My doctor did not ask me, but he told me, "Wheeler, I'm going to tie your tubes this time. You have a full house now. You have three queens, a king, and a jack, and that's enough for you." He was right. When I was told that my baby was a little boy, just what I wanted, I wondered how I could be so fortunate as to have three girls and then two boys. I gave thanks for my lovely family; I had just what I wanted, five healthy, beautiful children. I still feel that way.

My mother was very concerned; my father was becoming more dependent upon her to do everything for him. He had a pension, but she would have no income at all if he passed away. A girl working in Earle's office needed someone to care for her two children. I helped Mother fill out the papers necessary for her to keep the children, at least until she had enough quarters to get basic Social Security for herself in the future.

I told you, in the beginning I made a lot of mistakes. One was that I never made my children do anything around the house. My mother never let me do anything when I wanted to. I thought that when they needed to know housekeeping they could learn like I did. I know now that I was wrong. I wanted them to have music and to do well in school, and I did not want to take their time from what I considered the things that would serve them well in their adult lives. I continued to do all the housekeeping, cooking, and laundry. Needless to say, I stayed tired all the time and was still concerned about our income for the future.

I had been working for quite a while, and I kept up with the trends in nursing. The hospital nursing programs were beginning to close due to the fact that there were more opportunities for women after World War II. If I were to continue to work, I would need to work toward getting a B.S. in nursing to improve myself and my income. Just before William was born, I took my credits from Textile to the University of South Carolina and learned that I would have to take one history course, and I wanted to take English grammar. This would allow me to get into the studying mode again. In 1957, I took the English course, and the next semester I took the history course. I would go to school in the mornings and continue to work from 3:00 to 11:00 each afternoon.

We brought William home, and, sure enough, he did just fine with the other children. I stayed home for a short while after William was born. We had a very busy household. There was school, some were taking piano lessons, and others were involved in various activities.

One morning just before Christmas, we were having breakfast, and at that time we ate our meals sitting down together. It was very noisy, and I was franticly helping everyone when the doorbell rang. I opened the front door to find a woman I had never seen before, holding a small decorated Christmas tree. It seems that she was going to ride to work with Earle, and he had forgotten to tell me she was coming. Talk about a shock!

Katy was thirteen years old when William was born. She had been going to see the Little League baseball team play at a park near us. One day, she came home with a uniform and told us she was now the bat girl for the team. She was so thrilled. We thought that was pretty good since we had never heard of a girl doing that.

I told each of my children when they reached seven years of age that they would take piano lessons for three years. They would practice every day, and there was no need to ask to quit; there would be no quitting. I have always felt that music was part of a well-rounded education. After the three years were up, they could continue if they wanted to or quit. When they became adults, if they wanted to play, it would be easy for them to pick it up again. Katy took music the longest, and Ann majored in music in college. Sarah Jane didn't seem to like it that much. However, she did play the French horn for awhile. Smitty later played exceptionally well, and it helped him so much when he went through a very difficult adolescence. When the three years were up for William, he switched to guitar since that was the big thing going on then.

As for me, I was playing the piano almost every day, with a child sitting in my lap most of the time. I sang a lot and especially enjoyed playing and singing the old gospel songs. My children often asked where I learned them. They had not heard them in the Lutheran church. I learned them from my mother, who sang all the time and had had a good voice when she was young.

Katy tried to tell the teacher how to teach from the time she was in elementary school. Several times I had to be in conference with a teacher or principal. One high school teacher called to tell me that Katy wrote the best English paper he had ever seen, even though he had been teaching for years. Katy wanted to play in the high school band, and she chose to play the clarinet. She brought it home and practiced over and over one weekend, only to find she had learned to play it with her hands in the wrong position; so she had to unlearn all she had worked on. You will be interested to know that Katy became a schoolteacher and worked later with some of the same teachers who had taught her.

Ann also played in the high school band. She chose the French horn and enjoyed music very much. Later she also liked to play basketball. The teachers always wanted to compare Ann to Katy, but they were so different that that didn't work at all. Ann had a much different personality, very easygoing. She had lots of friends and didn't care too much if she didn't excel. She had other things she wanted to do, which was very much how I had been.

Sarah Jane, too, had lots of friends and was in the Girl Scouts, which she enjoyed. It was hard for her to follow Katy and Ann. For her, being the middle child was very difficult. However, she was very special to me. I told her she was my baby girl, and after Smitty and William were born, she asked, "Will I always be your baby girl?" I told her that she would be, and I was glad to be able to tell her that. Once we had a new United States flag, and I thought the best place to display it would be outside of Sarah Jane's bedroom window. Then she asked, "Can I be in charge of the flag?" My answer to her was, "Of course you can."

Everyone loved Smitty. He was a good child and spent most of his time with his paternal grandmother and her husband. All the old men at the church loved Smitty. Everyone knew he was extremely smart. He played Little League baseball, and later, when he was older, he umpired the small kids when they played. I did not like it when he umpired, because I had to listen to doting mothers criticize him many times for his calls. But since I was working, I didn't get to go very often, anyway.

Smitty joined the Boy Scouts. He had always been interested in my work, so he worked very hard to earn the first aid badge. I went to the Court of Honor so I could pin it on him. I was devastated when the program ended and his name wasn't called. As people were leaving the church where the program was held, I went up to the Scoutmaster and told him he had missed recognizing Smitty. He didn't seem too concerned. I was so hurt for Smitty and disappointed for myself. Needless to say, he chose not to continue in the Scouts.

When he was chosen for the National Honor Society in high school, I was there, and things went well. I was very proud of him. Later, the principal called and wanted to talk to Earle and me about Smitty. He suggested that we enroll him in the University of South Carolina early and that it was a waste of time for him to take the last year in high school. We did as he suggested.

William was a very good quiet little boy. He spent a lot of time with my parents after they moved across the street. It is always amazing how different children can be. Of course, I recognize that they can have traits from some long-ago ancestor the parents never even knew. William did well in school and music, but, like Ann, he had other things he liked to do. He tried Little League baseball, and he played in the field. Once during a game, a ball was hit toward him, but he was looking at the ground and didn't see it. Later we learned that there had been a very special insect on the ground that he was watching. So he didn't stay in baseball for very long. He just was not interested. He liked to read, and he wore out two sets of World Books because he read them constantly.

As you can see, we had a very busy household. With the rest of our family across the street, I seemed to be constantly on the run. Every holiday, Easter, July 4, Labor Day, Thanksgiving, and Christmas, I prepared dinner for everyone, including Earle's widowed aunt, who also lived across the street. She never had any children, and she loved Sarah Jane. So everyone had their favorite child to indulge. This extended family was referred to as "the grandmothers."

# Public Health Nursing
## 1961-1966

Just as I realized that I was going to have to change my future with more education, my body was giving out. My back and legs were giving me a lot of trouble, and I knew I was not going to be able to continue the strain of private-duty nursing very much longer. After a great deal of praying and considering other options, I received a call from an older nurse I had known. She told me that Dr. Brodie, the health officer for the Lexington County Health Department, wanted to talk to me. I met with Dr. Brodie, a wonderful man, and accepted a job with the health department in 1961. Dr. Brodie had been a chemist with DuPont before he studied medicine. There were three nurses in the department, and I was the first one hired in thirteen years. These three had worked together for all those years, so it was not easy for me.

I had worked private duty because each day was complete unto itself. My thinking was that if I had an emergency at home, I could always give up the case and be off. Public health was different. I would have a salary with vacation and sick days, and the process was ongoing. I never knew that public health touches the lives of everyone in one way or another, and a lot of federal money is used to protect the areas being served. It was overwhelming! I thought I would never learn it all. But after a probationary period and a lot more praying, it all fell into place.

We met every Monday morning in Lexington, the county seat, for the staff meeting. Lexington was just a small town; at noon, everything closed down, and we all went to Hite's, the one big eatery in town. All the county officials, lawyers, construction people, and a tourist or two were there, so it was a great time to catch up with the latest news. My specific area of the county was on the east side, and my hours were 8:30 AM to 5:00 PM.

The state had some special programs for citizens in need, including: heart program, crippled children's program, tuberculosis monitoring, prenatal and postnatal checks, and immunizations for children and adults in our outlying clinics. We were also familiar with the other health resources in the county and state. All this included home visits if they were necessary. I was fascinated with the scope of the service, and I really did enjoy it, so I put my whole self into it.

One morning after I had been working there for about a year, Dr. Brodie called me into his office. He told me that he had been watching me. He thought I had a lot to offer in public health, and he wanted to help me finish my degree. I was thrilled that he made the offer. The problem at the time was that I had to sign up for a chemistry course. I could make the class, but the lab was in the morning, when I would be working. Dr. Brodie offered to let me take four hours one morning a week of annual leave to meet the lab requirement. I was so excited and thankful, and I told him so!

The supervisor was pleased for me for having the opportunity, but the other two staff nurses were not pleased at all. The next semester was pretty difficult; they avoided me and were very cold if they came in contact with me. I said at the time, "I would rather be asked to leave than frozen out!" But I stuck it out, and three years later, I was so happy I did. I was never cold or rude to them; it's wrong. I treated them the same way I wanted to be treated. I knew God was with me while I was going through all this.

About this same time, we decided we had to have another house. Our little house, 1,200 square feet, just wasn't big enough to accommodate seven of us as the children grew up. I told Earle the decision would have to be his, because I could not tell my parents that we would be moving out of the area. I told my parents that Earle said we had to have a bigger house, and it went over all right. We sold the first house and built a much larger house but not a very expensive one; it just had more space.

In 1959, we moved into the larger house at 401 Lawand Drive in the St. Andrews section of Columbia. Gee, it was nice to be able to spread out. In fact, I would get tired of walking all over the house; it was so much bigger than the other one. I soon realized that I would have to have help to keep this big house, and William was only two years old.

The nurses in the health department told me about a black woman who lived in my area of the county who was really good and said I might be able to get her. I interviewed Juanita Suber and hired her. I could do that now since I had a steady job with regular hours. Juanita worked for me for seven years and was like one of the family. At that time she worked all day five days a week for twelve dollars a week, which was the going rate at that time. I raised her pay twice while she worked for me.

Let me tell you about some of my experiences working in a public health generalized program. The work was so varied, not at all like one patient each day. Most of the cases involved not just one person but the whole family. In this case, the problem was a three-year-old boy who did not talk. When I visited, he looked like a bright little boy with big brown eyes. After several visits, I learned that the mother was from the city of Boston, a high school graduate, and a Roman Catholic. She had married a young man from rural South Carolina, also a high school graduate, and he was Southern Baptist. This made for many obstacles for the family. What I found later was that the mother had never talked to the little boy. I had to teach her that children learn to talk by listening to others talk, primarily the mother. I visited them regularly for quite a long time. The little boy started making sounds and soon was able to talk. Another baby, a little girl, was born on my birthday while I was working with the family.

Another case involved a young mother as well. The family, very poor, lived in a small travel trailer out in a rural area. She was married and had a new baby about two months old. As soon as I went inside the trailer, I was overwhelmed by the smell of urine. The whole place was a wreck, but public health nurses are not used to seeing everything in perfect order; that is often why they visit in the first place. We rarely carried anything into a home. I sat down in a straight-backed chair. As I talked to this young mother, I saw huge brown roaches crawling up the walls, across the ceiling, and back down. I don't think I have ever seen roaches as numerous or as conspicuous. I kept wondering how I could tell this young mother that her home was infested with roaches. I would hurt her feelings and ruin any chance of being able to help her. I wanted to be very tactful. I admired the new baby for a little and then I said, "Are you aware that your home is loaded (simple word) with roaches?" Her answer, "Yes, but I don't know what to do about it."

This opened the door for a lot of teaching and helping her to have a better, more sanitary home. This was the beginning of many visits; she was ready and willing to learn. Later, they bought a house and had another baby. But I shall never forget that first experience.

We did have a nurse's bag filled with all kinds of things that we might need, but in the bag also was a large piece of newspaper. If the bag was needed in a home, it was always placed on the newspaper. There were strict procedures we had to follow when we visited a home. I was glad I did not have to take the bag into this home.

Many people see nursing as a depressing, serious profession, and it is sometimes, but there is another side I'll tell you about. One very cold, rainy day, which we do not have often in South Carolina, I got up early, prepared breakfast, and helped the children get their things together and get off to school. After cleaning up the kitchen, I saw that I was running a bit late for work. I hurriedly put on my uniform, combed my hair, and lightly made up my face. I went flying out the door, jumped into the car, and headed for the health department. When I arrived and looked at my schedule, I saw that I was to visit another woman that day. The area had unpaved streets, and water was standing everywhere as the rain poured down. I carefully went up the steps and knocked on the door. A voice said, "Who is it?" I replied, "It's the nurse from the health department." Next I heard,

"I ain't up yet!" Now it was about 10:30 AM . I remembered all the effort I'd made to get to work, and I couldn't help but think, *And I'm here to help her!* Well, that's how it goes sometimes. Some days were like that, but most were not, and I thoroughly enjoyed my work in public health.

During the sixties, our country went through a complete upheaval. There was the assassination of our president, John F. Kennedy, in 1963. President Kennedy and his beautiful young wife, Jackie, brought such a change to quiet fifties. Finally, here was a president who was born in the twentieth century, which seemed to signal a real plus for our country. There were student riots in colleges across the country, and illegal drugs were flowing freely. Riots occurred in the cities, and block after block was burned due to the people's unrest. Later Robert Kennedy, the President's brother, was a candidate for the presidency, and he was gunned down while campaigning in California in 1968. He was a friend of the poor, and his candidacy seemed to promise a better world for all. As if these two tragedies weren't enough, Martin Luther King, Jr., leader of the civil rights movement, was also assassinated in 1968. It seemed to me that things might not settle down for a very long time, and they didn't.

My family was going through its own upheaval. Katy finished high school in 1962 and entered Newberry College that fall. Her boyfriend, Eugene Bain, who finished high school at the same time, entered the University of South Carolina. Imagine our surprise when in November of that year, Katy came home and told us that she and Gene had recently married in Georgia. Both were seventeen years old. It was hard for me to believe this could happen, but it had. Now was the time for us to rally around them and see what we could make out of it. I knew we needed to talk to Gene's parents, but Earle told me he thought I should talk to Gene's dad. When I arrived at his office, his mother Sylvia was there also. They were more disturbed than we were, I do believe. I explained how upset we were, but I offered some consolation. Neither Gene nor Katy was typical of their schoolmates. I told his parents that we would help them all we could. I told them also that they would finish their education, but I could tell they did not think that would happen. Then again, they didn't know me, I would "make a way."

Dr. Chester Bain was employed at USC in a very important position, and I'm sure it was humiliating for him that his son married at seventeen. Soon he left Columbia to take a job at Emory University in Atlanta, Georgia. They lived in Atlanta for seven years. So it was left to Earle and me to do what we could to make the marriage work.

Katy could no longer live in the dormitory at Newberry, but a woman who lived nearby let Katy rent a room from her to finish the semester. Katy and Gene stayed with us for several months. Gene got a job with Slater Food Service, which provided meals for the university. Katy got a job with the telephone company, so both of them went to work.

They applied for an apartment in Hendley Homes, a federal project that housed students. Later, they did get a small apartment. Then I went to Sears and bought basic kitchen items, curtains, and necessities for a decent life. I helped them get settled, and life went on.

In the fall of 1963, one year later Katy and Gene had a small wedding in our Lutheran church and continued school until they both had master's degrees. They retired after living in Saudi Arabia for thirty years both working for Saudi Aramco. Now they live in a beautiful home in Ashburn, Virginia. They have three professional children and seven grandchildren.

In 1963, Earle's father died suddenly from a heart attack. This changed a lot of things for us. Earle was his only heir. Later, we learned that he had about $100,000 in the bank, as well as a housing development that consisted of a number of lots and a large, beautiful lake. This was not the best thing to happen to Earle; he immediately thought he was "rich." It took quite a long time to get the inheritance straightened out. I urged him to continue to live like we had been living and use the money only when it was needed. But he immediately decided that he wanted to build houses and sell them. He said, "I can do it, but you will have to help me. I can't do it alone." I had just gotten accepted into school and had been in public health for about two years. Based on his past record, I told him there was no way I could help him, continue to work, and be responsible for the family. However, he went ahead but did not have the knowledge to make it work really well. He soon realized that after he lost some of the money. We decided that we would sell a lot each time we needed money for the children's education. Their grandfather would have liked for us to use it that way. This worked out well, so he found another job.

After I had completed my chemistry, history, and English courses, I was ready to go to school fulltime to complete my degree. I had found out that there was money available for nurses to go to school. I made an appointment at the new nursing school at USC and talked to the dean. I told her about myself, and she said, "You have a husband and five children. Why do you want to go to school?" I told her, "It's something I have to do." She did not give me any encouragement at all. I went home and cried as I cooked supper. A friend of my husband came by and saw me crying, and I'm sure he thought we'd had some disagreement. He asked me why I was crying, and my answer was, "They won't let me go to school!" He thought that was pretty funny. I didn't think so!

But God had other plans for me, and I did get the scholarship to attend for one calendar year. I started in 1963 in summer school. After the first session of summer school, I learned that I had to have a hysterectomy. I had a very small window before the fall session. I told the doctor this, and he told me not to worry; he would have me standing in line for the fall semester. Sure enough, I was there.

Of course, I didn't have much free time while I was in school. I told Juanita, "I want you to know if someone comes in here and says my house is dirty, I will tell them that it's Juanita's house, not mine." She liked that and then really took over, and that was wonderful for me.

In June of 1964, I received my B.S. in nursing. I was not an A student, but I had already worked for twenty years, and I knew my job well; so for the amount of time I had, I did all right. The purpose of the scholarship was to improve nursing service, and I was always trying to do that.

Ann graduated from high school and that fall entered Columbia College, a women's college at that time. Ann wanted to major in music, and the university program was not as good as the one at the college. Ann stayed at home for two years and lived in the dorm for one year. Burt Jordan was at USC getting a doctorate in English. He was the head of the staff at a camp in New Hampshire during the summer. He met Ann, who had just competed in a diving meet. He hired her to teach diving at the camp the following summer. When she returned home, we learned that she and Burt were dating and planned later to be married. Ann and Burt married in May of 1968. One of my best memories is planning Ann's wedding. She had a large wedding, with all her friends from the college as her bridesmaids. After the wedding, the reception, as was the custom at that time, involved punch with various cakes, mints, and so forth. I had written to Burt's family and told them that the wedding would follow our Southern customs.

European immigrants did not come to the South for two primary reasons. South Carolina was an agrarian state, which meant we had little or no manufacturing, and the weather was extremely hot in the summer, before air-conditioning. Our history of having slaves came about primarily due to the fact that Europeans did not know how to grow crops in the South, work in the heat, or tend to an abundance of land to raise capital. So those of us who were reared in the South had never been exposed to descendents of other cultures. Burt and his family were of Armenian descent. Like others in that part of the world, having a wedding, a party, or a celebration of any kind is full of food, laughter, and drinking.

On the night before a wedding, the rehearsal party is usually given by the groom's family. Burt's family, and there were many of them, stayed at the Holiday Inn, and they served a lavish meal with their traditional flair. Again, I knew there were cultures that were very different from ours in the South, so I was not intimidated at all by their dinner and other plans for the evening. I've often wondered what they thought of the punch and little cakes.

After the wedding, Ann and Burt went on a cruise for their honeymoon. They went to New Hampshire to work at the camp that summer. In the fall, they found an apartment for the next school year.

After they both finished their schooling, they moved to Maryland so Burt could go to dental school, which was his goal. Ann taught music in a junior high school. Later, Ann became pregnant with twins, a boy and a girl. The little girl was stillborn, and the boy died in an accident in 2006. She later had a daughter, Emily Ann, before they divorced. Ann became a surgical nurse and is still working part-time in Australia and Atlanta, Georgia.

Just after Ann's wedding, Sarah Jane announced she was pregnant. She was in the eleventh grade. She had been dating a young guy for some time. Earle disliked him intensely, which, of course, made Sarah Jane that much more determined to see him. We all discussed options, but they wanted to be married, which we agreed to. We had a small wedding in our church for Sarah Jane and Dennis Dunlap, with a small reception at our house. The principal at Columbia High School gave Sarah Jane permission to attend adult school so she could finish high school before her baby was born in December. Dennis went to day school and worked for his uncle, who ran a cleaning establishment. They lived with us that school year. Their little girl, Dawn, was born on December 30, 1968. Sarah Jane had a very difficult delivery, and it took a long time for her to regain her strength. Now I had another little one in my house. She was a darling little girl, and we loved her so much. When school was out, Dennis and Sarah Jane found a garage apartment and moved. When the baby was nine months old, my front doorbell rang. When I opened the door, there were Dennis and Sarah Jane holding the baby. Dennis said, "I've brought Sarah Jane home with the baby. I don't want to be married anymore." They got a divorce, and Sarah Jane and Dawn lived with us until Dawn was three years old. Sarah Jane finished college in 1972 and has been teaching at a high school for about thirty-five years. Later she received a master's degree and is now diligently working on her doctorate. Dawn married and has three children. Sarah Jane later married Jay Byars who also teaches at B-C High School.

***

While I was going to school fulltime, my only thought was to return to Lexington County and continue my job there. But that was not meant to be. The staff nurses there told their superiors that I could not come back, because they did not have degrees and that would put me over them. This is the staff that tried to freeze me out, and this time they did, but in a different way. Since I was paid with federal money, the State Department of Health could assign me wherever they wanted me to be. Their decision was to assign me to the Richland County Health Department. I was given the title of Maternal Child Health Coordinator.

In this job, I was in charge of all the clinics: prenatal, postnatal, family planning, and child health. These clinics opened at noon each day. Scheduling, setting up the rooms, keeping records, and following up with recommendations were not problems. But one thing posed a problem for me personally. I had to go to lunch each day at 11:00 AM, which meant that I could not eat with the other nurses or actually feel like part of the staff.

Many of the patients came from rural areas and rode into town with their husbands when they came to work. That meant they were at the health department all day when they had to attend the clinic. After I'd become familiar with the program, I talked with the health officer about starting the clinics at 1:00 PM instead of noon. This would accommodate the women so they did not have to sit in the waiting room all day when they would be seen for only about twenty minutes. If they had to see the clinician, it would be longer by about another twenty minutes. Best of all, it would permit me to have lunch with my colleagues, and the women would have some time to do something else if they so desired. The answer I received was that these women looked forward to coming to the clinic and that they did not mind sitting in the waiting room all day. So that was that.

Several nurses in this department had already received their degrees, but they did not have much work experience. Since I had been nursing over twenty years at this time, I was sent with them to outlying clinics on several occasions. Once we went to a clinic and found the place filthy, certainly not what one would expect for anything promoting good health. I reported this to the health officer, and he asked me, "Do you know how to mop and clean?" I said, "I mop and clean at my house, but I haven't gone to nursing school to mop and clean."

Sometime later we were sent to this same place again. It was a very cold day, and everything was frozen. We had no water nor bathrooms available, the building was cold, and so were we. Again I reported this, but there was no concern about the situation.

In Lexington County, we had a janitor who would go the day before to an outlying clinic, turn on heat or air-conditioning, and clean the place. When the nurses arrived, we were ready to start serving patients. It seemed so simple. In one place the man in charge had compassion for the patients; in the other situation, there was no compassion or even any concern. That did not go over big with me.

One day while I was working, I was called to the phone. It was the assistant superintendent of Brookland-Cayce School District (B-C District), whom I knew. He told me the district was going to hire a nurse and asked if I'd be interested. I said, "I'll take the job!" I never even asked about the salary; I would just be pleased to work in Lexington County again. The two staff nurses in the health department had recommended me for the job. This proved that it wasn't me personally they did not want in the health department; it was the difference in ranking. I was pleased to know this, because I really liked both of them. I worked at the Richland County Health Department for two years.

When I resigned, my consultant in the State Department visited the Richland County Health Department. We had a meeting with the health officer, the supervising nurse, the consultant, and me. She said, "Is there anything we can do to make you stay here?" I said, "No, I'm sorry. This isn't a Christian place to work, and I do not want to be here!" She was such a lovely, gentle lady, and she drew in her breath and said, "Why, Emily!" That ended that. The Health Officer had shown no concern at all about the working conditions for the nurses nor did he even care about the patients we served.

After John F. Kennedy was assassinated, Lyndon B. Johnson became president. He was always concerned about the poor. He signed the Civil Rights Act into law in 1964 and anti-poverty legislation the same year. This was part of the program referred to as the "Great Society." As I write this, I see that it is no wonder that the country was in turmoil again. But out of all this came new programs to improve the situation of those who were less fortunate in an effort to bring them into mainstream American life.

One such program was the Elementary and Secondary Education Act. Under the act there were many programs listed as Title I, Title IX, and so on. Nurses were hired by boards of education under Title I to work with the schoolchildren who qualified for the services. There was a strong health component under Title I. I was paid with federal money under Title I when I worked at B-C schools.

# School Health
## 1966-1975

Public schools in South Carolina were still segregated in 1966. There were fifteen white schools and two black schools in the B-C District, with a total enrollment of twelve thousand. Almost every child in the black schools qualified for Title I benefits, and in the B-C District we also had a large number of white children who qualified. Nan Thompson, who was hired as a social worker, and I started work on the same day in 1966. I was asked if I could train Nan in social work. I told them I was not qualified to train a social worker but that I would teach her what I knew about working with families. Olive Bennett was the reading specialist, and the three of us were housed in a small brick house called Special Services.

I designed the health program to reach all the special children and to provide for the others as well. I recruited, trained, and supervised about 250 volunteers each year. The volunteers did vision and hearing screening in specified grades each year, and I would rescreen those who needed follow-up. Some volunteers staffed the health rooms in the schools. We were not permitted to administer any medications in school, according to the State Health Department, which provided our guidelines. At this point in time, we did not have many children who had to receive medication. That came later.

Each year, I taught the Red Cross First Aid course twice, and it was open to teachers and parents. I spoke often at PTA meetings to give parents information about the programs. I had a referral form and held in-service meetings to help the teachers identify problems in children and refer them to me. I visited homes and set up appointments with doctors and dentists as needed. Nan took the children to their appointments if the parents were unable to do so. I spoke on various topics, showed films, and used various teaching tools.

As is typical for me, I took several courses on teaching the disadvantaged, adult education, and teaching and serving handicapped children and adults.

Each semester, a professor at USC had me speak to his health education class. The B-C program was unique, because I had designed it and implemented it. Most of the time a person will design a program and someone else will implement it.

Nan and I worked twelve months each year. The Head Start programs were started as six-week programs in the summer to prepare children for school in the fall. I pretty much used the same approach as during the winter months, but all of these children qualified for health services. I visited many homes and did the screening myself. Later the Head Start program ran year-round and had its own facility.

The school nurse consultant was in the Department of Health. She became my good friend and came over often to see the program. She encouraged all school nurses to join the South Carolina Nurses Association (SCNA). We could form our own section and receive information on national concerns and available resources. Most of the nurses did join. I was elected chairman of the School Nurse Section, SCNA.

After I had been with B-C schools for seven years, our consultant in school health left the state. I liked her so much, and I hated to see her leave. The lady who said, "Why, Emily!" when I left Richland County called me and made an appointment to visit me. She offered me the position of Consultant in School Health for South Carolina, and I accepted.

Around 1972, a master's degree program in nursing had been established at USC. Because I had been so involved with health and education in the state, I was asked to consider transferring from education, where I had earned quite a few hours. I hand-carried all my papers and transferred to nursing. I went one semester and was totally frustrated the whole time. I was not happy and did not like the way the program was set up. After that semester, I picked up my credentials and went back to my advisor in education. He knew me and said, "Emily, I could have told you that you have been in public education for too long to go into that kind of program." I guess that was the reason, but I didn't belong there for sure. In 1974, I received my master's degree in education for exceptional children. It was about all handicapping conditions, as well as the gifted and the mentally retarded. It has served me well.

I need to back up now and bring my marriage up to date. You know the circumstances of our marriage. When we married, both of us wanted it to work out well. Earle had a plan for what he wanted to do; it was no secret that he wanted a good wife and children. It was the custom for wives to do what their husbands wanted them to do. For the first years of our marriage, I tried to do what he wanted me to do in the traditional way. But as things progressed, that just wasn't feasible. One of the first things was that we could not share a checkbook. He never kept records or remembered what he had done, and finally it was better for each of us to have an account. He paid for the mortgage, groceries, and utilities. I paid for clothes, music lessons, and incidentals for the children. He did lunch money. So we shared, but we always knew how much we could spend. Earle could not focus on a career and did not try to improve himself in any way. For example, he would decide that he wanted to landscape the yard. He would go to a nursery and buy lots of plants and bring them home. He might plant two or three, and then he was unable to finish. I used to joke that it looked like he'd been struck by lightning. The tools would be lying on the ground where he had been planting. I would pick them up and put them in the garage. I didn't mind, but that practice does get old. Early in our marriage, we had nothing, and neither of our parents had money to help us. We were like many other couples at that time. Most people had very little because the Depression was just rebounding, so people were saving a lot and spending as little as possible. Each time Earle was fired from a job or tried to do something that required self-discipline and failed, he became depressed. When I would come home from work, he wanted me to sit and talk to him about his childhood. He said I was his psychologist, and perhaps that was the help he needed. One time, a doctor gave him some antidepressants to help him. He took them for about a week, and he felt better; then he thought he didn't need them anymore. This happens often with patients.

In 1969, after Earle had been working for seven years at an insurance company, he came home early one afternoon. It seems he had done something and was fired on the spot and told to leave immediately. I couldn't believe it. He said the worst thing he had ever had to do was tell me. Well, we had to go through the cycle again. I have no idea how long we went through the same things we had gone through so many times before. I had responsible jobs now, and I really found it hard to take care of everyone and do my job, too. I realized for the first time, although I didn't say it out loud, that I could not go through this many more times. By now I saw my marriage as something very difficult, and I wondered if it was worth saving. But I still had Sarah Jane; her daughter, Dawn; Smitty; and William living at home. There was just no time to evaluate my marriage.

Meanwhile, across the street, my father's health was deteriorating, so the doctor put him in the hospital. My mother was no longer able to care for him at home. He was mentally clear, so I explained to him that Mother could not care for him, and he told me, "Just put me in one of those homes." It makes such a difference when a parent can make his or her own decisions regarding their care. It was not that way with my mother, but that comes later. My daddy was in the nursing home for over two years before he died in 1973.

Smitty entered USC in 1971 and graduated cum laude in mathematics in 1974. When we talked about his future, he told me that he was going to be a doctor. I encouraged him to have an alternate plan, because sometimes it was hard to get into medical school. It was sort of traditional in South Carolina for a doctor to send his son to medical school so he could take over his practice when he retired. But the medical school took Smitty before he had graduated from college. Smitty decided he wanted to be a pathologist, and Yale had the best program in the country; he was accepted there. It was very difficult for Earle and me to accept how exceptional Smitty was. After his residency, he went to Naples, Florida, and worked for the hospital there for three years. Ann was living in Naples at the time. Smitty had a chance to join a group in Phoenix, Arizona, and he is now chief pathologist and director of laboratories at St. Joseph's Hospital. Later he became a commissioner for the American College of Pathology and now travels all over the world checking laboratories. Many foreign countries want to have the same standards that we have in the United States. Smitty was married for several years, and they had a daughter in 1982.

After I accepted the position of consultant in school health for South Carolina, I wrote a letter to the state superintendent of education, who just happened to be the person who hired me to work at B-C schools. Schools try to be very aware and careful about who comes into the schools for any purposes other than those approved by the administration. Perhaps this had not been done before, but I wanted to have his support before I went into South Carolina schools. He appreciated my letter and responded favorably.

When I reported for work at the Department of Health and Environmental Control (DHEC), I was ushered to a small cubicle, which would be my office. That was fine; I was new and had a lot to learn. I stayed in this job for two years and was moved four times. The head of the division seemed to have trouble placing me anywhere. There were four other consultants in this section of the division, but they all worked with the county health departments. Maybe he just didn't think I should be in his division at all. I know personally from early experience that his arrogance might have been pricked when I contacted the education office, or maybe he just didn't like me. I have always had a strong personality but know how to handle it well. Anyway, I travelled around the state, so I wasn't in the office very much. I had learned years earlier to concentrate on my job only and not to interfere with other workers in whatever they were doing. I enjoyed my job very much, and one reason was that I knew it so well. I had had so much experience working with educators and understanding them. It was hard for the school nurses hired at that time under Title I to understand how to be supportive of education. I worked hard on that, and some were able to make the change, but some never did.

In 1972, while I was still working for B-C schools, the school nurses wanted to nominate me to become the president of SCNA. I was flattered that they felt that way about me, but, of course, I doubted that I could win the election. But they persisted. When I went home, I talked to Earle about it and reminded him that it would mean some overnights to visit other parts of the state and more demands on my time. He thought it was great that the nurses felt that way about me, and he encouraged me to give my permission; so I did. Earle always supported me in my work. Perhaps he remembered the condition we'd agreed upon before we married.

I'll never forget the election. My opponent had been a director of nursing in a hospital in Columbia for a very long time and was widely known; I wasn't sure about myself. True, I had worked in a doctor's office, did general duty in a hospital, did private duty for a number of years, and had been a public health nurse, a school nurse, and a school health consultant. I guess it all counted, because politicians say name recognition is most important. I won the election, and I was so overwhelmed I could barely speak.

For many, many years, hospital nurses had pretty much controlled the organization, and here I was, a sort of renegade, since my master's degree was in public education. The people I worked with were always my friends; I truly loved them, and they seemed to feel that way about me. I have always been a strong supporter of nursing. I served one year as president-elect and two years as president of SCNA. I have a strong leader personality, and everything the board wanted, we were able to accomplish while I was president. I served as president from 1973 to 1975.

After Earle lost his job in 1969, it took a while for him to find another. Until he finished high school, he had visited Columbia to see his mother, so he'd known a lot of people for a long time. After he began to work again, he decided that he wanted to build us another house on the property his dad had left him. We looked at books of plans, and the only lot we wanted was one that had a view of the lake. However, it was a strange lot. When the dam had been built for the lake, the dirt had been taken from this location, and it was really "a lot in a hole"! After the whole family had reviewed the plans, we ended up deciding on a very large A-frame house. When the planning was going on, Sarah Jane; her husband, Michael; Dawn; Smitty; and William were living with us. We thought that the large house would be perfect for everyone.

After the house was under construction, Sarah Jane decided that they wanted to build a house for themselves. Earle had told the children that each one could have a lot if they wanted it. We lost three of our tenants right there. Then Smitty left to go to medical school in Charleston. So that left the two of us and William. In 1974, we moved into the large house at 133 Collumwood Circle, West Columbia, South Carolina. I had hired an interior decorator to help me pick colors, carpets, drapes, and other pieces for the new house, and she did all the legwork. It was really beautiful when we moved in.

William was a rising senior when we moved, and that meant he had to go to Lexington High School for his senior year. He did not like this, but everything changed so suddenly that there was nothing that could be done. William graduated from high school in 1976. He went to USC and received his B.S. in engineering in 1980. There were two tracks in engineering: power systems and computers. William took the computer track. He has worked a number of jobs, though this is not because he was fired. His first job was for the military at Warner Robbins Air Force Base in Georgia. From there he went to Connecticut, where he worked for Timex, but they soon stopped making computers.

Then he went to Colorado and worked for various companies over a seven-year period. He married Maria Gorgey in 1985, and they have three children. They moved to Saudi Arabia for five years to travel and save some money, and then returned to Columbia. William now works as head of data systems for Ag First Bank in Columbia.

I began to see some serious changes in my mother not long after my daddy died. I visited her once a week for lunch. She always enjoyed my visits. On one visit, she bragged that she had saved me a piece of chicken and fried it for my dinner. When I bit into the chicken, I realized it was badly spoiled. I hated to tell her; she was so happy that she had prepared it especially for me, but I could not eat it. I blamed it on the grocery store; maybe it had not been labeled properly.

One day, she phoned me, and while we were talking, she started screaming and left the phone. I called Earle's mother next door, and her husband, Ingram, answered and said he was just about to call me. It seems that a frying pan with grease that was on the stove had caught fire. Ingram saw the fire from their bathroom window, ran over to my mother's house, and put the fire out. Lurline told me all about it, so I immediately went over to see about my mother. I knew she could not live alone anymore. It was just not safe for her.

We talked about it, using the safety factor as the reason she had to give up her home and live where there were people to care for her. Of all the things that happened in my life, this was, and still is, by far the worst. Everything I accomplished came from the way she'd reared me and directed me. I'd watched her live a life she did not like because she was a married woman in a time when there were limits on married women. She was so proud of me, and I wanted her to be proud of me. I knew there would be a lot more ahead for this intelligent, beautiful, and oh-so-smart woman.

I contacted Mrs. Rikard's nursing home, where my daddy had spent over two years, and explained about my mother. They had a bed, and I could bring her over the next day. We got her things together and prepared for a temporary stay at Mrs. Rikard's.

My mother had polycythemia vera, a condition that involves all bone marrow elements. It is a lifelong condition, but she was not diagnosed until she was in her late sixties. In her case, she had an overproduction of red blood cells. There is no cure for it, and the cause is unknown. The treatment was to remove some blood periodically to keep the red blood cell count low. However, when the blood was reduced, it took all the other elements with it; so to correct a prolonged condition, it took a long time, with many pints of blood drawn. Today, there are other treatments that can be tried.

Prior to this emergency situation, Mother had complained to me often of various ailments. She was seeing a medical doctor regularly, and the symptoms were present, but he missed or just overlooked them. So for years the red blood cells had been building up. She had trained at the state hospital and often said to me, "I think I'm losing my mind!" As her blood became thicker, it was unable to pass through the capillaries of the brain, and she had intermittent periods of confusion. Some days when I visited, she would be fine; but other times, her behavior would be quite different. As people grow older, we assume that these symptoms can appear, and since she was being seen by a medical doctor, I had no way of knowing that she had this problem for many years.

My mother had been Lutheran since her marriage to my father, so she wanted me to contact the Lowman Home near Columbia. I talked to the superintendent about a boarding room for her, but we had to wait a while. The day I was to call him back, I had been working out of town, but I stopped at a rest area and used a pay phone. He said very calmly, "We have a room for your mother." I burst into tears I was so relieved. This would be a permanent move.

The Lowman Home had a lovely dining room that we looked at on our first visit while making plans for Mother to live there. But in a month or two, when I went to see her, she wasn't eating with the other ladies; she was sitting at a cubicle, enclosed on three sides. It upset me terribly, but I was told that she would take food from the other residents, so she was no longer able to sit at a table. Later, she was moved to the next step, which was intermediate care in another building.

Before I left town for four days for a pediatric conference in another state, I went by to see my mother, and she seemed to be doing well. She knew I was going and said goodbye. When I returned to Columbia, before I went home I went to see about my mother. She was sitting up in a wheelchair and said she was ready to go back to bed. I rolled her into her room and pulled back the blanket that had covered her legs. I was totally shocked to see that one leg was almost black all the way to the knee. I said, "Mother, look at your leg! Has it been like this before?" Her answer was, "Oh, yes. It will get better when I lie down."

There was no licensed person on duty. The law required a registered nurse for only one shift at that time; it may be different now. I went out to the nurses' station, told the person on duty what I had found, and said she must get the floor supervisor to check my mother the first thing the next day. Not surprisingly, she called me the next morning before I left for work and told me my mother was on the way to the doctor's office. I met her there. After his examination, the doctor announced that Mother would have to have an amputation. The surgery was scheduled for the next morning at 7:00. My head knew it the day before, but my heart just wasn't there yet.

The next morning, I was at the hospital at 6:00 AM. I talked to Mother, and she seemed all right, but in retrospect I don't believe she knew what was going on. Then she was moved into the holding area. The nurse in the waiting room called me over to sign the permit for the surgery. I told her, "There is no way I can sign that permit," and again, I burst into tears.

She was very compassionate and tried to reason with me, but that wasn't to be. Then she said, "You need someone to be with you. Would you like me to call your husband?"

"No, he couldn't help."

"How about your minister?"

"Not him, either."

"Who can I call?"

I said, "You can call Dr. Milling. He is a family friend."

When he was on the phone, she called me over, and he said, "Now, Emily, you know your mother will die if she does not have surgery."

I did know that, but I said, "The nurse will have to give me something, or I can't do it." He ordered a sedative, and sometime later I did sign the permit. In about an hour, he came to the waiting room to see about me and stayed for a while. I appreciated him so much and told him so. I had never felt so alone in my life.

I wish I could tell you that everything went well. But it did not. After waiting for three hours, I had the nurse check on the situation. She reported back that the surgery had not been done yet. It seems that a patient came into the E.R. who was bleeding profusely, so Mother was pushed back. Sometimes that happens. By now it was noon, and Mother had been without food since the night before.

Finally, the surgery was completed, she was out of the recovery room, and the day was over. I could not believe it when I learned the doctor had amputated her leg below the knee. If you remember, her leg was already black to the knee when I first saw it. Two weeks later, she had another amputation, to mid-thigh.

Oh, there is more. In about six weeks, mother's other leg had to be amputated, and the doctor did it with two surgeries. He did the lower leg first, and two weeks later he did the upper leg. The only positive thing I can say is that I don't believe Mother ever knew that her legs had been amputated. No matter how bad things get, there is always a light moment, and I'll share two of those with you.

When Mother first went to the Lutheran home, each time I visited her she would say to me, "I can't believe you took me out of my home and put me here. When can I go back home?" That's when we have to learn to give evasive answers. When the permit had to be signed, I could just hear her saying to me, "I can't believe you let them take my legs off!" She didn't say that, but she did say, "Emily, I want to go shopping."

"Why do you want to go shopping?"

"I want to buy a pair of shoes."

"Why do you want shoes?"

"What do you think I want with them? I want to wear them!"

Then I knew she did not realize that her legs had been amputated.

Another interesting thing happened. My granddaughter Dawn who was about seven years old at the time, used to go with me to see my mother. After the amputations, I was preparing her for the visit. I said, "Now don't say anything about Mother not having any legs."

She asked, "Doesn't she know she doesn't have any legs?"

Humor hides so many pains.

My parents attended Reformation Lutheran Church in Columbia for twenty-two years before they moved to the country. Mother was involved in all the women's projects to raise money for a young congregation. When they moved across the street from us, she went to church every Sunday. When Mother died on December 5, 1975, one of the ladies who was in the group with my mother called me and said, "Emily, we can't do anything for your mother's death, because Mrs. Glover died the same time, and she was a charter member!" That was absolutely the last straw. My mother was gone, but inside I was hurting for her, because she loved that church so much.

My mother was buried beside my father in the plot in Elmwood Cemetery that Earle and I had bought when his father died.

After my mother's death, I had to clear out her house and dispose of her personal things. This is always very difficult, and I didn't have the luxury of taking my time, because I had to return to my job. Gene, the boy my parents reared, came to help me. He was able to take most of the furniture to his house. I didn't have any room since we had just moved into a new house and everything that was needed had already been purchased. The house belonged to Gene and me, and later he bought my half, so I no longer had that responsibility.

# Instructional Television

## 1975-1977

I had been working at the State Department of Health for about eighteen months when Harvey Teal came to see me. He was employed by the South Carolina Department of Education Office of Instructional Television & Radio, which was housed in ETV in Columbia. We had a lovely visit and all my dealings with educators had been very pleasant. I did not know Harvey, but he wanted to talk to me about doing a series on health as part of the life science course offered to middle-school children. I listened carefully as he outlined what had been envisioned for the program. I was thinking that he would want me to promote the series in the schools as part of my work. Then he surprised me: he wanted me to come to work for them and write the program! I told him I knew nothing about writing for television, but he insisted that I was the person they wanted to do it. This was a complete shock! Here was God rescuing me again from another unhappy situation.

I assured Mr. Teal that I would give it some thought and get back to him. On the way home, I kept thinking, *What in the world is happening?* I didn't even look at TV very much, and writing for it was foreign to me. More important, could I do it? Mr. Teal had been so reassuring, but he had said he couldn't find anyone else. I thought he must be mighty brave to want to take a chance with an inexperienced person like me. Honestly, it threw me for a loop!

I knew my present job inside and out, and things had been going really well. The nurses were happy working with me.

Earle and I spent several hours talking about the offer that night. As usual, he encouraged me to take the job and told me I could do it. I thought, *That's easy for him to say.* However, the job would take about three years, and there would be very little travel. I prayed about it and received the encouragement I needed to undertake this new project. All the jobs I had taken were covered under the South Carolina Retirement System, and taking this job would be a lateral move under the State Employment System. My salary and benefits would remain the same. In a few days, I called Mr. Teal and took the job.

Those I worked with were shocked that I would leave the hallowed halls of health to go to work for lowly education. As I told you earlier, it's an ego thing. People would sometimes ask me which I'd rather work for: health or education? My answer was, one is run by doctors, and the other is run by people who love working with children. What do you think?

So in May of 1975, I went to work for the State Department of Education, and my office was at ETV on Millwood Avenue in Columbia. The State Department of Education is located in downtown Columbia in a high-rise. I was to be at work at 8:30 AM. When I got there, I was bewildered that no one else was there. That was the first thing I learned—and I liked it. This was an office of creative people, and I am sort of one of those, as you will see. You are hired to do one thing, and you do it your way. You have to constantly be thinking and/or dreaming of what you want to accomplish, and you do it in the best way for you. When I walked down the hall, I would see people just sitting at their desks or looking out into space, and I knew creative thinking was taking place. You did not have to be sitting at your desk to write; you could do that wherever it was most productive for you. The big thing was, you were on your own. You had a job to do, and they depended on (trusted) you to do the job the best you could in whatever circumstances worked best for you.

I kept saying to myself, *I wish I knew how to do it, or what I'm supposed to do.* Others said, "You'll know soon." So I waited. But I prayed all the time while I waited. I knew this was for middle-school children, so I became familiar with the contents of the textbook they would be using so I could complement it. Then I needed a format, so I had to ask myself a lot of questions. I would be doing twenty-five fifteen minute lessons, and I had to write the teacher's guide. As a trial program, I wrote one on vision and hearing using middle-school children as characters. It was okay, but then I began to get a feel for what I wanted to do.

At that time on commercial TV, detectives were popular, so I decided I would use a detective, and he had to have a car. I chose his name. He would be Jason Conrad; Jason, which means "the healer," and Conrad, "giver of wise counsel." My director decided Jason would drive a yellow VW beetle. By looking at the textbook, I determined what I wanted to cover, and then I planned the sequence of lessons. At least then I knew what I was supposed to do.

My title was Instructional Specialist, and there were four others. One was doing a social studies series, another a reading series, another history, and the other was doing some things in music. Each specialist had a TV director assigned to her or him. So we really worked independently. My director was Tom Shirk. I was responsible for the content's accuracy, and he was responsible for making the programs as innovative and interesting as possible. I was told that the instructional specialist and the director were like a married couple; we had to work well together to make sure we produced a really good product.

Tom and I became very close friends, and he worked a lot like me—sort of "fast and furious"! Later, when I left South Carolina for twenty-eight years, Tom was the only person I had worked with who stayed in touch with me. I really did appreciate it.

I wanted to use characters with dialogue in the series. The health instruction would be given by the characters Tom had selected. I used medical school textbooks to be sure I had accurate information. Each lesson could stand alone, so if a teacher wanted to use several of the lessons, he or she could; or if he or she wanted to use one lesson, that would work, too. The teacher's guide included activities for all ability levels. If you remember, my master's degree in education focused on exceptional children, and it, too, included all teaching levels.

"Conrad" could be used in any classroom for one lesson or twenty-four lessons. Later, we learned that the students loved the series. The series was distributed by the Agency for Instructional Television and used in the United States and Canada. Tom and I were pretty proud of our work on the series.

While I was working on CONRAD, a Charleston school district received a federal grant to prepare a TV series to teach teachers how to use paraprofessionals in their classrooms. I was asked to write the three twenty-minute lessons and a teacher's guide. I named it *Teaching Another Dimension*. I wrote the material to be very upbeat for the teachers, but I had nothing to do with the production. After it was produced, I found that the director had not picked up on that part, which actually made the material much more entertaining as well as informative. I had no say in that part. I never knew how well the school district liked it. So many things for teachers are pretty dull. I hope that one wasn't too bad. It could have been so much better. Tom and I could have really jazzed it up!

I had never thought of myself as a writer, but after I went to work at Instructional Television, I found that I loved to write. There were no computers then, and I found that the words would pour out of my head faster than I could write. It was a talent I didn't know I had. Some nights when I went to bed, if I was working on writing something, I would just lie still with my hands folded over my chest. If Earle said anything to me, I would say, "Shhhh! I'm writing!" I could see the written page in my head and could rewrite and change all kinds of things without ever putting anything on paper. It was another God-given talent I didn't know I had. I really enjoyed my time at ITV, but there's more. I had a terrific experience I want to share with you.

When I was living in Houston, I went to a barbeque supper given by our church. When we were standing in line waiting to be served, I started making small talk with a young man standing in front of me.

"Are you a member of our church?"

"No, but I used to be when I lived here."

"Where do you live now?"

"I live in Dallas."

Pause.

"What kind of work do you do?"

"I could tell you, but you probably wouldn't know about it."

"Try me!"

"I work for instructional television."

"You're kidding! I used to work for ITV a few years ago."

"Then you know all about it, right?"

"I sure do. I worked in South Carolina for about two years as an instructional specialist. We do quite a bit of production. Did Texas ever use any of our productions?"

"Yes, we did. In fact, there was one I really liked."

"I don't know them all, but which one did you like?"

"I really did like CONRAD. I watched it."

"Really? And you really liked it? I wrote and helped produce it!"

"I can't believe this!"

"My name is Emily Davenport now, but I was Emily W. Collum when I did CONRAD. You've really made my day!" And he did. What a nice young man! It was really a thrill for me. The series was used in the United States and Canada. It made some money for the state.

\*\*\*

After all the writing was finished, Tom did the production, and of course I had to be present to make sure he did it like I wanted it done. We had to go on location to Atlanta for the road scenes with Jason driving the Beetle, and other locations for different parts of the lessons. At that time, all the portable cameras were powered with wet cell batteries, like automobile batteries. When we arrived at our destinations, everybody, including me, grabbed up stuff and carried it to the location site. It was lots of fun and work, and we enjoyed it.

Tom and I were told that we'd completed the series in the shortest time ever. After it became available to schools, I went to various places in South Carolina to explain to the teachers how to use the programs and activities.

During this time, an older nurse I knew called me and said that George Rentz, the president of the new Lexington County Hospital, would like to talk to me and asked me to make an appointment with him. As soon as I had time, I made the appointment with Mr. Rentz and went to see him.

I had known Mr. Rentz professionally, but not very well. He was very forward-thinking in his idea about the delivery of healthcare in Lexington County. You remember how I liked Lexington County. We talked for quite a while as he outlined what he wanted for the hospital in the way of health education for doctors, nurses, other staff members, and patients, as well as the community, for the prevention of hospitalization. I thought it was an ideal plan, and I told him so. He wanted me to write the program for him on a consultant basis. I agreed to design the program for him as he had described it to me. This was going to be some extra money for me, and I was very excited about his request.

It did not take me long to design the program. I enjoyed doing it and found I had another talent that had been hidden way down deep somewhere. After I finished writing the program, I took it to Mr. Rentz, and he was very pleased with the plan. He later presented it to the board, and they wanted the program just as I had designed it and would pay whatever it took to get it underway. One catch: they wanted me to take leave from ITV and come to the hospital to get the program started.

# Lexington County Hospital
## 1977-1979

At ITV, they wanted me to write another program for high school students, and I had already done quite a bit of research for it. So I had a dilemma. I wanted to do both, but that was not possible. I was having problems at home since Earle was out of work again, so I asked ITV If they would let me take a year's leave to go to the hospital and get the program started; then I would return to do the high school series. They agreed. So in May of 1977, after two years at ITV, I left and went to work at Lexington County Hospital.

Two people had already been hired for the Health Education Department when I arrived. One was a young man who was functioning as director of health education, but he lacked the knowledge and experience to do the job, and he knew it. So he became the media person, because that was his preparation. The other was a young lady who was the librarian. Our department was housed on the ninth floor of the original building. The library and media equipment were housed on the first floor. I had a lot of contacts who were interested in being part of this innovative program. I hired a secretary, a staff educator, a community educator, and two nurse educators. Later, I added a public relations man and a secretary for him. Everyone I hired was very experienced and knowledgeable about community resources. In a very short time, we had programs up and running. Mr. Rentz and I saw this style of organization as a good way to integrate the disciplines rather than having different departments doing their own education. When each department made up their budget, they had a category for education. The money each department built in their budget was all lumped together, and that was my budget. It seemed so sensible and efficient; there was a specialist available to cover each of the different departments, and the production of print and audio/visual needs was covered under education.

The program I designed was so unique that I wrote an article that was published in *Hospitals*, the official magazine of the American Hospital Association. In addition to that, I wrote a piece for *Resource*, which is their publication dealing with training in hospitals.

While I was working at the hospital, I received a list of courses that were being offered in the fall by The National Endowments for the Humanities. These courses were for a month for doctors, nurses, and others who worked in hospitals. My secretary looked at it and brought it in to me and asked that I make a selection, just to see if I would be accepted into a course. I selected medical ethics based on the history of medicine, because I like to study history. This was going to be taught at the medical branch in Galveston, Texas.

As you already know, Earle was not working again, and we were going through the same old routine we'd been through so many times before. The idea that I might be able to get away for a month to rest and think about something other than work was very enticing to me. I filled out the application and sort of forgot about it.

Several weeks later, I was attending a meeting at a hotel in Columbia, and my secretary came to the door to tell me, "You're going to Texas!" This required me to rethink my priorities, but I knew I could work it all out. Finally, I would have a change, and it did me so much good just to know that there would be a brief break for me in about six weeks.

Mr. Rentz gave me permission to attend the seminar for four weeks. I think he could probably see that I was in a very bad condition from all the stress in my life. The staff in our department all knew their jobs well and were mature enough to carry on without having me there to oversee the day-to-day activities. I had swapped cars with

Earle, and I was driving our old Buick so he could use the other car to look for a job. I would be driving to Texas, so he decided I should have a new car for the trip. I bought a new 1978 Chevrolet Monte Carlo for about $7,500. It had black-and-white sidewalls and light trim. It was pretty sharp, and I enjoyed driving it.

Everybody at my office was very excited about my being accepted for the seminar. The Public Relations person was on board, turning out some excellent material. A nurse who had retired from the Navy came over from Sumter, where she lived two days each week, to be part of our special educational program. Mr. Rentz and I were both very proud of the way the program was evolving.

Sometime during 1977, while I was still at ITV, the situation at home had gotten worse. William was still at home and attending USC. Earle and I spent many hours discussing his being out of work, and slowly all the bills, housekeeping, washing, cooking, and car upkeep had passed on to me. I felt completely weighted down with all that was going on.

In May 1977, I started working at the hospital, and things at home were about the same. One day, I was attending a meeting at the hospital, and when we adjourned, my secretary came to me very excited. She told me that my husband had called me a number of times while I was at the meeting. She said that he did not sound good, and she thought I should go see about him. I hurried home, and when I went in, Earle came walking down the stairs. He looked terrible, and I realized that he was inebriated; I was very angry. He was not a drinking man at all. He had not had anything to eat, and I hurriedly prepared him some coffee and a sandwich. After he ate, he seemed to feel better. I told him I had to go back to work, because I had to preview several films to be used in a program the next day. He understood and said he would be all right.

I knew this sort of behavior could not continue for either of us. In the course of my work, I had referred several patients to an excellent counselor in Columbia. I called him for an appointment. When I walked in he said, "Hey, Emily! How are you, and how can I help you?"

I said, "How can you tell someone about thirty-three years?"

His answer was, "Just tell me what made you come today." From there, we went into an hour of discussion pertaining to my problems at home. Afterward he said, "You've been living this way for over thirty years?"

My answer was, "I don't give up easily."

"I can tell," he said.

The purpose of my appointment was to find out if there was anything I could do that would help things at home. He had no answers, but I went once a week for several months and then not so often for a full year. One time, I was in such a bad condition that my secretary drove me to my appointment. Earle knew I was going to the counselor.

Just before Christmas in 1977, Earle and I had a long talk. I told him I did not mind working and sharing my money with the family, the same as he'd done in our early years. However, I could not do that and everything else that had to be done at home. Since he was not working, I suggested that he vacuum, dust, mop, wash the clothes, and prepare some light food for us to eat.

He said, "I just can't do it." And I knew that he couldn't.

I replied, "Then I think it would be best for you to go and stay with your aunt."

He agreed and then asked, "Would you like to have a divorce?"

My answer was, "No, not now. We'll just have to see what happens."

I was in such a terrible condition at this time that I reminded Earle that all he ever wanted was a good wife and some children. I told him I had been a good wife and he had the children he wanted, but I could not give up my life for him, and he understood that. After the holidays, he went to live with his aunt, who had lived across the street from us in the early years. We separated on good terms. Neither of us was angry, and we continued to stay in touch.

In March of 1978, Mr. Teal from ITV came to see me to remind me that my year's leave would be up in May. Actually, I have to admit that I had thrown myself into getting the program started and had not really given any thought to the next year. So much had been going on in my life.

Harvey wanted to know all about the program. I told him there was one more piece that had to be completed before I could leave. That part was patient education that would be used on the closed-circuit television system that had been installed in the hospital. Some programs had been done, and I did the writing for those. He listened patiently while I talked on about the program. Then he calmly said, "You're not coming back, are you?"

And I remember my answer. I calmly said, "Not now."

He thanked me and left, and I felt bad; they did need the high school program badly, and I had wanted to do it, but for some reason I just couldn't see myself working there again. We don't always understand the plans God has for us, and He has always put me where He wanted me to be for some purpose. I did not know it at the time, but He had done it again.

I was now into my second year of working for the hospital. This is when I received the announcement, "You're going to Texas!" The seminar was in October. Earle was going to come to our house to stay while I was gone so he could feed my dog and make sure everything was all right. William was still in school. I loaded my new car and headed for Galveston, Texas. I have always loved to drive, and since I was only twelve when I learned, I am an excellent driver with a good driving record. Of course, I have received two speeding tickets, but I can explain those. When the speed limit was reduced to fifty-five miles per hour in the 1970s to reduce the consumption of gasoline, I was travelling then for the state; it was very hard for me to keep my speed down, especially on two-lane roads in the country where the traffic was light.

According to my map and the little I knew about Texas, it seemed to me that I should drive to Houston and then to Galveston. However, I stopped at a gas station before I arrived in Houston, and there I learned that you just take a road from I-10 and go right into Galveston. I still didn't know that Galveston was an island. Maybe everyone else knew, but I didn't. I followed the directions I was given but was really shocked when the road suddenly ended at a ferry boat landing. I wondered if I had taken the wrong road. But I acted like I knew exactly what I was doing and went dead ahead. Sure enough, I went by ferry across Galveston Bay and ended in the city of Galveston. Then, hey! I felt like an explorer who had just found a new land.

I had been given a list of places to stay. The first one I visited was not up to my standard, which is not that high. If you have rented at a beach, you know what I mean. Yes, the island had a beach. Imagine that: bay on one side and beach on the other. But I have to say, it was not a pretty beach at all; the beach is not white sand like those in South Carolina. Finally, I found a one-bedroom place with a nice little kitchen, and I chose it for my stay. The medical school was about three blocks away from the apartment.

We had a small party at the professor's house in the late afternoon. I was so excited about my experiences from the trip that I talked too much, which I do when I'm excited. They were ready to throw me out the first day, I think. There were twelve of us: ten practicing physicians, a chaplain, and me, the nurse. We had class all day, and at night we studied. Our weekends were free. Several of the men had brought their wives. I was very familiar with how things were in South Carolina, but I learned a lot from the other class members. Everywhere I go, I'm told that I talk a lot. I'm basically a happy person, and any new thing I learn is exciting to me. You must remember that this was in the 1970s, when nurses were still standing at attention in the presence of a doctor. One doctor was a psychiatrist, and he disapproved of me from the beginning. He never tried to hide his disapproval, either. He was the kind of doctor who would cause a little kid to stick out his tongue expressing his feelings toward him.

When I was living in Florida years later, everyone commented that I talked a lot. My friend Nora, who was reared in Nebraska, noticed something I never had noticed when I lived in South Carolina. When she moved up here, she told me that everyone here talked all the time just like I did. So it isn't just me; I guess you could call it a cultural thing. So what the heck: this doctor was from New England.

There were two female doctors in the class. One was a medical doctor from Washington State, and the other was a pediatrician from the Dallas area. I can't remember their names, so I'll call the one from Washington State Mary and the other one Ruth. The first weekend, Mary and I drove over to San Antonio and spent the night there. We visited the Mexican market and bought some things to take back home. Mary had flown to Galveston, so if I hadn't had my car, she wouldn't have had the opportunity to see San Antonio, which is a real treat. It's where Texans go on vacation.

You probably remember that my roommate at Textile in Spartanburg both years I was there was Ruby Thompson from Greenwood, South Carolina. She married Gerald Pearson, who was also in our class, and he was from Greenville, South Carolina. He served during World War II, and Ruby stayed with his family, because she was pregnant at that time. Twice on weekends when I was in nursing school, I went to Greenville to visit her, so I knew the Pearson family pretty well. Gerald's sister, Sue, visited us at school and stayed in the dorm. After the war, Ruby and Gerald married and settled in Houston, Texas.

By the time I was in Galveston, Gerald had died, and Ruby had married Joe Terry. They were living in Houston. On our second free weekend, I went to Houston to see Ruby and Joe. We had a really nice time reminiscing about our time in school. In the course of the evening, she told me that Sue, Gerald's sister, had died. She knew that Earle and I were separated. She told me that Gary "Red" Davenport, Sue's husband, was in the process of being transferred from Chicago to Houston. She told me all about him and ended with this statement: "I've never known two people so much alike!" She wanted us to meet each other, and she asked me if I could come back to Houston in a couple of weeks. I assured her that I would check my calendar and let her know.

I had no time until after Thanksgiving, so on December 6, I flew to Houston. Ruby wanted me to see the decorations and beautiful lights in the Galleria, which is a large three-story mall. The whole area was just beautiful. On December 7, Gary flew to Houston for the weekend; he was staying in a motel until he was able to move into the house he had just purchased. It was a strange night. Ruby prepared supper for us, he came in, and it was amazing. He told me later he had been praying so hard to find someone else and he knew when he saw me that I was the person God had sent for him. The chemistry was just perfect. We said many times that we could have married that night; we both felt the same way, that we were supposed to be together. Both of us were shocked, because we saw only each other. Joe and Ruby went to bed early, and we sat and talked and talked and talked. He said to me several times, "When you come to Texas to stay." Gary and Sue had been married for twenty-seven years, and Earle and I had been married for thirty-three years, so it wasn't that we didn't know what marriage was all about.

The next night, both couples went out for supper together. We had thrown Ruby for a loop. She'd been somewhat of a matchmaker for several of her friends, but she'd never dreamed that we would become a couple in one night. She asked me all kinds of questions, and it was plain to see that she was worried about us. She told me privately that she thought the four of us would just go out together and that maybe I could come back occasionally and it would be fun for all of us. But that plan had been altered. I left on Sunday, and Gary took me to the airport. Ruby was completely out of the picture. I guess you could say her work was finished, but God had completed the plan in a different way.

The first thing I found out when I got home was that our house had been robbed while I was gone. All my jewelry had been taken, including nursing pins, high school ring, my first engagement ring, a necklace Earle had given me the first Christmas after I met him, and all the silver gifts and pins that had been given to me when I changed jobs. One very special piece was a small diamond ring that my parents had given me when I was six years old. The strangest thing was that I had no past anymore. All I had was the jewelry I had taken with me on the trip to Galveston. I've always thought that God was testing me to see how important those things were to me. I hated to have the losses, but they were just things and could be replaced if I so desired.

The next day, I phoned Earle. I told him about the weekend, and I said, "You asked me if I wanted a divorce, and I told you no. But now I must tell you that I do want a divorce. I have met someone I want to go out with, and I can't do that while I'm still married." He understood and agreed.

I called a friend whose husband was a lawyer and went to see him. Getting a divorce in South Carolina was not an easy thing at that time. The law was going to change, but when that happened, there would be a backlog of people waiting; he advised me to go out of the country, which is what people were doing at that time. He suggested I go to the Dominican Republic. Many had been to Haiti, but due to the unrest there, he didn't want me to go. These divorces were legal in the States and were handled by lawyers in Kansas.

There were some requirements; no children could be involved, and all financial arrangements had to be resolved in the States. This had to be a noncontested divorce. All this was explained to Earle, and he agreed, so we proceeded with the signing of the papers. While I was in Galveston, Earle went to Lexington and deeded the large A-frame house to me; when he gave me the deed, I gave it back to him. I told him the house was too large; I could not keep it up, and I wanted him to take it back.

While all the legal work was being prepared for me, I went looking for an apartment. I found just what I wanted, a two-bedroom townhouse in the St. Andrews area in Columbia. I remember that Earle helped me move and get settled. The draperies needed to be changed, and I told the manager that I planned to be there for a long time so there was no hurry.

I was living there at Christmastime and I had lovely decorations including a beautiful tree. But as much as I thought my family cared about me, I spent the Christmas holidays alone. Tom, my director at ITV, had Christmas dinner with me. He was alone, too.

Gary's mother was an invalid and lived in Greenville, South Carolina with her sister. Gary came to Greenville during the holidays to see her and visit Sue's family. I met him in Spartanburg and spent some time with him. Nothing had changed, and again he would say, "When you come to Texas to stay."

Gary was working very hard since this was a new job for him, and in January he had to go to Chicago to get things ready to be moved to Houston. Every night, after everyone left the office, he would call me. We talked for hours and hours about everything. He knew I was planning to go to the Dominican Republic, and we talked about that. We talked about our likes and dislikes in foods and all other things involved with living together. I told friends later that we never did talk about the thermostat, which poses a problem for so many couples, but we learned later that we liked it at the same temperature.

In January, the divorce papers were ready, and we signed everything. The plans were made for me to fly to Miami and change planes for the remainder of the trip. Of course, I was going alone. On Saturday morning, I flew to Miami and boarded a plane for the rest of the trip. It was like a bus. People got on board with all kinds of things they had bought in Florida, carrying many bags and parcels. I found it very interesting. We arrived at the airport late in the day. There was supposed to be a man there who spoke English to meet me. I waited and waited, but no one ever showed up. I went to the information desk, and since many people came there to get divorces, I'm sure they knew why this American woman was there alone. I had the name of the hotel where I was to go. They found me a driver who did not speak English and gave him all the information so he knew where to take me. And off we went.

I have no idea how far it was; my guess is about thirty miles. We drove and drove, and the sun began to settle down over the water. It was a beautiful scene. But my only thought was that no one except my lawyer knew where I was. I didn't know where I was going, and I wasn't sure I would know when I got there. But I was never afraid. Gary and I were very strong Christians, and we felt this was all part of God's plan for us.

It was dark when we arrived at the hotel. There was a man there who spoke English, and he had been looking for me. He handled the transaction with the cab driver. After he gave me my room, he said I was to be at the lawyer's office at nine o'clock on Monday morning.

The lawyer's office was right off the hallway in the hotel. This was Saturday night. Remember, all this had been only one day.

On Sunday morning, I had breakfast at the hotel and looked around. There were people in the pool—this was January—and the area was beautiful, filled with green tropical plants. I asked the man at the desk if he could find me a cab driver who spoke English and who would be willing to take me sightseeing in the city. We had a great day! We went all around the city and saw some beautiful old churches. I learned that the Dominican Republic had had an uprising for some years; only during the last year or so had things really settled down, and now they were ready for vacationers from other countries. A lot of effort had gone into returning the city to its original beauty.

After we returned to the hotel, I sat by the pool. It was so beautiful and very peaceful. I saw two couples in the pool who were American.

On Monday morning after breakfast, I went to the lawyer's office. From there we walked about a block to another building and went upstairs. The two women I had seen in the pool were already seated. My lawyer told me where to sit. The courtroom was small, and we three women and our lawyer sat on one side of the room. On the other side was another lawyer who was sitting alone. At the front of the room were several windows. Like everywhere in the tropics, there were no glass panes and no screens. They had wooden shutters that could be closed for hurricanes or extreme weather. It was easy to hear the sounds from the street outside.

The judge came in, and we all stood; when he was seated, we sat down. He pounded his gavel and started the proceedings. He explained the procedure to us. We had our lawyer with us, and he introduced the other lawyer, who was representing our husbands. He called one of the other women. She and our lawyer walked to the bench. They exchanged some words, and the other lawyer had no comment. So like that it was over for her.

I was called up next. My lawyer walked up to the bench with me. It went like this:

"Are you Emily Collum?"

"Yes, sir."

"You want a divorce?"

"Yes, sir."

He looked at the other lawyer and asked, "Is everything in order?"

"Yes, your honor."

He looked and me, pounded the gavel, and said, "Divorce granted."

That was all there was to it. It was over. Then the other women went through the same procedure. We all left the courthouse together and returned to the hotel.

After I had everything together and checked out of my room, I walked out to the pool area and talked to one of the other women. She told me they had both been there before for divorces. They were from New York and had tattoos on the exposed parts of their bodies. They had brought the men they were going to marry with them, and they were going to spend a week at the hotel. They told me I should have brought my intended husband with me. I felt so puritanical and tried to imagine how I had gotten into this kind of situation.

Two days after I got home, I learned that Mia Farrow had just divorced Andre Previn in the same courtroom. Just think: I could have been there with the celebrities. I can tell you this, it was quite an experience. I just read in the paper recently that in South Carolina you can now get your application for a divorce off the Internet, and it costs only $150. Someone told me you have to be separated for a year before you can apply. I was glad Earle and I had been separated for a year before we made that decision.

Around February 18, I returned to Houston. Gary had moved into his house. He never asked me to marry him; it was just a foregone conclusion we'd come to the night we met. Two days after I arrived, he announced, "When I come home for lunch, we'll go get the blood test," which was a Texas requirement.

Gary had promised his boys that if he married again, they could be there. I thought about Sarah Jane and Dawn, who lived just down the street from me; I felt very close to them. However, I reasoned that Sarah Jane was almost thirty years old, and she did not need me to babysit Dawn anymore.

God had "told" me that he had something better for me. I had given all I could give to Earle and my children. It was time for me to have something for myself. So Ruby and Joe got busy, and on February 22, 1979, Gary and I married in the Memorial Street United Methodist Church in Houston. Only the four of us were present for the wedding. The church was just half a block from Ruby and Joe's house, so we walked there. Afterward, they had a small wedding cake for us, and we toasted to our lives together. Ruby, Joe, and Gary are dead now. Only I still survive.

# Starting a New Life in Texas
## 1979-1989

After we had the wedding party, Gary and I went to Chili's Restaurant for a chili burger. Every year on our anniversary while we lived in Houston, we went to Chili's, and they would give us a free dessert. On our tenth anniversary, when we went to Chili's and told them we were leaving Houston and moving to Florida, they gave us a free meal as well as a dessert.

Houston commemorates its special past around the last twelve to fifteen days each February. About fifty miles from Houston, groups are formed to ride horses, pull wagons with supplies, and drive all the way to Houston. It takes about a week for the trail riders to congregate near the Astrodome. There are rodeos and a cattle show and sale, with lots of food and dancing. It is a tremendous event, and Houston residents look forward to it each year. All of this was going on when Gary and I married. Since we were new to Houston, we were just overwhelmed with all that was taking place. We decided at the time that people in Texas really know how to enjoy themselves and that we wanted to be part of it. We had grown up in a very conservative state where older people did not do much but church work, cooking, eating, and keeping house. Much later, as we travelled around the state, we found men and women in their eighties dancing the two-step and the polka.

We spent lots of time talking about putting our lives together. Gary's furniture had already arrived in Houston, and the house was full. Of course, there were boxes everywhere. But everything had to wait until I returned.

I flew back to Columbia to give two weeks' notice that I would be leaving. Everyone was surprised that I had married since I had always been such a traditional person. I was never one to take a chance with anything. The same was true for Gary. As I have said before, both of us were surprised at what had taken place, but it was as if we were supposed to be together. This was what God had intended for us, and we never looked back.

The weekend after I returned to Columbia, Gary came and spent the weekend with me to meet my friends. They gave me a party, and Mr. Rentz from the hospital came, he told me later, to check out my new husband. He was pleased after he met him. The hospital gave me a lovely silver tray that was engraved beautifully with names and dates.

I had to tell the manager where I lived that instead of being there for an indefinite period of time, I would be leaving in six months. Earle helped me pack to move, and he felt sure I would be coming back. I took my piano, a lounge chair, my sewing machine, my father's rocking chair, one bar stool, and the dishes I could take in my car. I left a lot of my clothes, books, and other things. Since the house we had lived in was home to my children, I left it just as it was. Earle and William were living there since I had been living in my townhouse.

It was my intent to start over and make a new life for myself. None of the things I owned meant anything to me. I was fifty-five years old, and I was sure this would be the last time I would have the chance to start over. Not many people ever want or need to change their lives, but I had worked so hard, taking care of everyone and picking up the pieces when things fell apart, that I knew I had to have some peace. God reassured me that this was what he wanted for me, so I just pressed on. All my children were grown, and some had children of their own. I felt that if any one of them had a problem, they were old enough and mature enough to handle it themselves. They did not need for me to "fix" everything for them anymore. I had been blessed with very smart, capable children who had reminded me many times that they did not need me.

I went to see my counselor, who wanted to know about everything, and he was very encouraging. I told him, "I feel like I've died and come back to life! I think this must be like the Resurrection." We need never fear when we move from one place to another. God is always with us if we let him be a part of our lives, but it is totally up to each of us to make that decision. I had made that decision in 1941.

Benjamin Gary Davenport, Jr., or "Red," was born on November 14, 1925, and reared in Greenville, South Carolina. He was an only child. His father died at a rather young age, and later his mother married again. Gary did not care for his stepfather at all, and I think he disliked his mother for marrying him. He was a very private person and never talked about his parents or stepfather. It didn't matter to me, so I didn't ask. He loved his Davenport grandparents. His grandfather was a Baptist preacher and had a number of churches in the rural area around Greenville. His father was in very poor health and was unable to work for long periods of time, so Gary spent a great deal of time with his grandparents. As was the custom, someone from the church would ask Rev. Davenport and family to their home for Sunday dinner. Invariably, they fried a chicken they had raised on their farm. Gary told me he would never order fried chicken in a restaurant because he had eaten so much of it when he was growing up.

A lot of these times were during the Great Depression in the 1930s. People tried to raise all the food they ate. My family always had a huge garden and a flock of chickens. We had fried chicken frequently on Sunday, as well as chicken and dumplings, smothered chicken, roasted chicken, and chicken prepared many other ways. It was the way people in South Carolina lived. I really enjoyed fried chicken and did not care how often we had it for a meal. I still get hungry for it every now and then. I've never been able to cook fried chicken like my mother did, but the chickens are not like the ones my father raised for us, either. Oh, how he loved his chickens!

It was very difficult financially for most people during the Depression years. The Davenport family was poor, and Gary's mother went to work in a cotton mill when her husband could not work. There was somewhat of a stigma toward those who worked in the mills. It was mostly because many workers had no formal schooling and had left their farms, because the land was farmed out. They found an easier way to earn a living.

Gary was a good student, and he told me he often taught math in high school. He graduated from Georgia Technical College in industrial engineering. I don't know how his education was funded. He told me once that he had an appointment to the U.S. Naval Academy, but he had to have $100 for books; there was no way for him to get the money, so he could not take advantage of the appointment. That was how bad it was during that troubled time. He worked in the cotton mill during the summer to earn money for school. He loved machines and loved to hear them hum, clang, bang, or whatever sound indicated that they were working properly. Remember this, because I will come back to this point.

During World War II, Gary enlisted in the U.S. Navy and was training to become a pilot. Part of his classroom training was at the University of North Carolina. He had just flown his first solo flight when the war ended and he was discharged.

After he finished college, he married Sue Pearson, who was also from Greenville. Sue graduated from Baylor University in Waco, Texas. Her major was home economics. Gary and Sue had four children. Ben III, who finished his degree at Lamar University in Beaumont, Texas, retired from the U.S. Navy and now works for the National Security Administration near Fort Meade, Maryland. William Kirby also retired from the U.S. Navy is an operator at the nuclear power plant near Dothan, Alabama, where he lives. Susan Davenport, who finished her studies at the University of Illinois, is now in Fountain Hills, Arizona. Their youngest, Ann Marie, was born with cerebral palsy and died when she was twelve years old.

I'm afraid I can't give you many details about Gary's career. He worked in Virginia for Dan River Mills and was the engineer for a cotton mill in Union, South Carolina. From there he decided to leave the textile industry for Westinghouse Corporation to work with electrics. He first went to Pittsburgh, Pennsylvania, then to Buffalo, New York. After that, he spent ten years in Chicago, Illinois. It was in Chicago that he lost his little girl and his wife. Then he was transferred to Houston and was in the process of moving when I met him.

After I had worked my last two weeks, I was ready to leave Columbia and return to Houston. I was very excited and wanted to drive the whole distance in one day, which is over nine hundred miles. I called Gary, who told me I must spend the night and come the next day. I stayed in a motel room in Slidell, Louisiana.

The next day, I was up early, ready to continue my drive to Houston. Fortunately, the weather was beautiful, or maybe it just seemed that way to me; I'll never know. Checking the mileage, I had told Gary I would be there by 3:00 PM. I arrived at the house at exactly that time. I thought he would be there waiting for me, but no. I don't think he wanted the people in his office to know that I was coming that day, so he worked until his regular time.

I had a key, and I went into the house, which was filled with boxes full of goods from his home in Chicago. He had unpacked his personal things and had them in place. Of course he had taken up all the closet space with his clothes. He had left *one* drawer in the dresser for my clothes. I have to give him credit: he had the kitchen things unpacked, and the kitchen was ready to go. I'm sure most men would have done the same since cooking and eating is so important to them. Gary had been used to Sue and Susan's cooking, which was outstanding, but cooking for me was having enough good food for my family to survive. It was not one of my talents. In fact, Earle had teased me about my cooking all the years we were married. He always said I was the only person who could cook breakfast bacon and have it be burned on one end and raw on the other. It was just one of my lesser talents.

When Gary came home, he was very glad to see me, and we unloaded my car. I asked him where he thought I was going to put my clothes. He gave me a blank look, like he'd never even thought about it. We laughed as he went about shuffling things so I at least could hang my clothes in the closet. The drawer situation was cleared up later.

Our courtship had been quite a bit different from what one would expect. As you know, we talked for hours and hours on the phone. We discussed our likes and dislikes in foods, movies, books, and other things involved in everyday living. I was so glad to learn he was not a sports fanatic. We seemed to like the same kinds of things. His hobby was photography, and of course mine was writing. That worked well for us, as you will see. He was highly competitive, which I was not. He'd been an A student and really worked to be the best at what he did. I, on the other hand, had not been an A student.

When I was in nursing school, the director talked to me several times about having better grades. I always had to please myself. I didn't care if everyone made better grades than I did. I have always loved going to school and learning in whatever form it took. Learning was never work for me; it satisfied my inquiring mind. Whenever I started a new job, I would look for a course that would increase my knowledge on that particular subject. When it came to putting this knowledge to work, I was always at the top of what I did. That is why so many people looked for me to take on a position that could broaden my abilities, and I loved the challenge.

We lived at 3104 Kingsbrook Lane, Missouri City, Texas, 77459. Missouri City is a suburb southwest of Houston. Our community was Quail Valley and was not too far from the Westinghouse office where Gary worked. Gary had bought the house before he met me, but I loved it. It was located on the sixteenth fairway of one of the golf courses in the development. He told me he'd bought the house there because he had planned to play a lot of golf. Just as my life had changed dramatically, so had his.

Gary went to work every day before 8:00 AM and did not come home until after 6:00 PM. So I was home all day alone. The only people I knew in Houston were my roommate and her husband, who were about forty minutes away. I hadn't realized how much I needed all this alone time. I was so exhausted that my hands shook so badly I could barely write legibly. I don't remember ever having time alone, so I used this time to rest my mind and my body. I noticed gradually that I was getting much better mentally and physically. We ate out often, so I didn't have to cook or do many household chores for quite a while. I read quite a bit; however, most of the time I just sat around thinking and trying to put my life in order.

When I went back to Houston after we were married, I was surprised that Gary had already established a joint bank account for us; he had changed all the information at Westinghouse, as well as everything that legally needed to be changed. I remember well the first time I wrote a check on our account; my hands really did shake. It was the first time I had written a check for money I had not earned myself. He told me also that he wanted me to be in charge of the checkbook. All of this was surprising to me, because he really didn't know me that well. But I'm sure Ruby had given him good references.

Sue's family had said that Gary was a strong male chauvinist, and they wondered how he would like to be married to a strong career woman. Well, in short, he loved it. I think more than anything it was a real challenge for him. He had been the strong one in his marriage, and I had been the strong one in my marriage. But both of us were willing to give to and for each other. I'd like to tell you about two things we had to work out.

When the Davenport family left on trips, it was Gary who checked the house to make sure all the lights were off, the thermostat was set correctly, the locks were on, and the house was in order to be left for a week or two. At my house, I was the one who did all of these things. Early in our marriage, we noticed we were going around behind each other doing the same things. So I called his attention to this, and then we agreed on who would do what.

The other thing was just so funny to me. We had decided that we wanted a wrought-iron patio set for our covered patio. Gary loved to shop, so very often on his lunch hour he would wander through stores just looking. Imagine, a man who loves to shop! He told me he had found a nice patio set, and he wanted me to go see if I liked it. The next day, I went to look at the set he had seen. The store was close to where we lived, which was rare in Houston. I liked the set too. When he came home, he asked if I had been to the see set. I told him I agreed that it was a very nice set. The next day, he went to look at it again and noticed something he hadn't noticed the first time. He wanted me to go back and see what he was talking about. So I did. Would you believe he went back again the next day? When he came home, we went through the same thing again. He wanted me to go back to the store. Then I knew what the problem was: neither of us wanted to make the decision for fear the other would not approve. So I took the bull by the horns, so to speak, and said, "You like the patio set, and I like the patio set, but I refuse to go back again to see it. Either you or I should go up there, buy the set, and get it delivered. No more of this kind of stuff." That took care of the problem. I'm sure he made the decisions in his family, as I did in mine. When it came to getting things for our house, Earle wasn't interested; he just left it to me, and that was all right with me.

In the meantime, while I was getting myself together, the boxes that Gary moved to Houston were still sitting in the middle of the floor in every room except the kitchen and our bedroom. Of course, I had shifted some of them to make pathways to get to things that we needed. But I asked if it was all right if I started to unpack the boxes. I knew full well that he was waiting for me to do it. I knew what he wanted: for me to be a wife and make a home for us, and for him to be the husband who would go to work. So I thought I best get started on my project.

I've told a lot of people, "If you think unpacking things after you move is a job, you should unpack things that belonged to another family and have been moved into a new home." But, undaunted, I took over. I was glad Gary had unpacked the kitchen; I think that's a hard part of moving. It was so interesting to see that the Davenport children had had many of the same things as the Collum children. Gary loved music and had taped many of his selections from records, so I put on tapes and had entertainment while I worked. I loved the recording of "Georgia on My Mind" and played it over and over. I stayed in most of the time, because I was not familiar with the area where we lived, and there were no sidewalks. I certainly had plenty to keep me busy. The house had been a model, so it already had lovely window treatments. In a couple of months, I had everything in place, and we could start thinking "outside of the house."

The first thing we talked about was where we wanted to go to church. I was still a Lutheran, and Gary had grown up Southern Baptist. Right at first, he told me he would be glad to go to a Lutheran church if I wanted him to. There were few Lutherans in Houston, but we did visit a Lutheran church, and we agreed it was just okay. Then he told me he had been going to church at First United Methodist in downtown Houston, which is a huge church. At one time the pastor had been the chaplain at Georgia Tech when Gary was in school there. I'd always liked the Methodist church, and the college I attended in Spartanburg was a Methodist school. After I visited the Houston church, I agreed we should join there. Since it was such a long drive to church, we did not participate in the many activities that took place during the week. We continued our membership there until we left Houston ten years later.

Ruby always said when new people move to Houston the first thing they want to do is learn to square dance and the second is learn Spanish. Bill, a man who worked with Gary, told him that he and his wife, Norma Jean, went square dancing at least twice a week. After we had the proper information, the next Tuesday we went to the meeting and found out they were starting a class right away. Of course, we signed up. I have played the piano all my life and always had a lot of rhythm. I had always wanted to learn to dance, just ballroom dancing. Square dancing is very old, but it used to be very easy to learn in a very short time. Not so now. There are so many complicated moves that it takes about a year to really learn it well. We promptly acquired the proper attire and became very involved. What fun it was, but difficult to learn. We never gave up and enjoyed it so much.

The women and the men dressed alike: she with her short dress over a crinoline skirt that matched his shirt and the towel that was hooked to his belt. Everyone had ID pins on their left side identifying the club where they were members, and each time your club visited another club, you received a pin from them. After a few years, we had a long string of pins on our chests. Since I could sew, I made all my dresses, one for each time of the year we celebrated—Christmas, Valentine's Day, St. Patrick's Day, and so on. I had about fifteen different dresses. We danced for ten years, sometimes two or three times a week. In square dancing, there are "tips"; there is a patter call first and then a song with words adjusted by the caller. Then there is a break, and we did ballroom dancing between tips. Gary and I never stopped dancing. I really believe that my good health is due in great part to the high-energy square dancing we did for ten years. In Texas, the movements were fast and, I might add, furious! After we moved to Florida, we went to a couple of dances, but it wasn't the same. Some of the people were so old they sort of walked through everything, and since there were more women than men, often women danced both parts. We didn't like that, either, so we stopped dancing. There were two levels of dancing above what we did, but we did not want to learn any more. Later, I gave away all my beautiful dresses!

During the first year I was in Houston, I spent my time getting adjusted to a new marriage, a new home, and a new city. But by fall I was beginning to think of work again. I contacted several hospitals in Houston to find out if they were doing anything like I'd done at Lexington Hospital. They didn't know what I was talking about. I should have guessed that; Mr. Rentz at Lexington was always very forward-thinking in his planning. The article I wrote that was published in *Hospitals* was chosen because it was so innovative. Now all hospitals and medical centers provide various kinds of instruction for the people in the communities they serve. But at that time, I couldn't make them understand what I was talking about.

One afternoon, I was feeling pretty bad because no one was interested in the kinds of things I had done. When Gary came home, I told him about my efforts, and he responded, "Why do you want to go to work? I told you I would take care of you. I make enough for both of us."

My answer was, "I have always worked, and I enjoy my work very much." He said it was all right, and he hoped I would have better success in the future.

I had done some continuing education for nurses in South Carolina, helping them learn to teach patients at home. Houston Community College had a Health Careers Center, so I went there to talk to the director. It so happened that the Visiting Nurse Association in Houston had written a program of enrichment for their home health aides, and the community college was to implement it. Again, God had sent me to the right place to find the very best thing for me to do. No one at the college had had any experience with public health, so I was perfect for them. There was one problem: it was funded by Medicare for one year only, and I would be using a curriculum written by HEW in Washington, D.C. The salary in the project was much too low for my background. I was surprised at what they offered.

This was September. The director said the salary was too low for a person with a master's degree, but if I waited until January, he would be able to give me more money. So I did not fill this position until January of 1980.

# Houston Community College
## 1980-1981

I was the director of the project, and I had a registered nurse, a nutritionist, and a home economist who worked with me. I taught communication and the psychological aspects of patient care. I studied the project and learned that the goal was to graduate seventy-five students. The classes were made up mostly of older black women employees of the Visiting Nurse Association who were involved in home health services. But two students were from another home health agency.

Alvin Community College is located in Alvin, about eighteen miles from Missouri City, where I lived. I visited the director there, and, with his help and some publicity, I had a class there made up of eight middle-aged white women. These women were not employed at that time but wanted to be prepared if they had the opportunity to be employed at a later time.

Since I was implementing a project that had been written by someone else, it was necessary for me to visit them to get a feel for what they had been thinking when the project was drafted. I was disappointed in what I encountered there. They were very surprised that I had so much experience, as well as a master's degree. They kept trying to impress me, but it was obvious to me that the organization was badly in need of help. They did not care for me; I knew too much. Later, they wanted me to teach the aides to do things that clearly violated the Nurse Practice Act, and I refused. I used the material prepared by HHS and adhered to the goals of the project.

Then they contacted Mrs. Jones, my boss. She went to visit them and supported me in my decisions. None of them had the education and experience that I had. When I returned from my first visit with the visiting nurses, I had told Mrs. Jones, my boss, that there were real problems in the agency. Not much later, she told me there had been a big staff turnover. I had seen that need immediately.

I was not prepared to be an "outsider" when I went to Texas, which is a Southern state, but that's what I was, and this was something I had never had to deal with. Obviously I was a threat to all of them. It provided another experience for me. Going to work in an established situation to implement something new or different is always a threat to those who have been employed there for some time. I have two rules that I adhere to at all times. First, I always talk to the people who are already employed and explain what I'm supposed to do so they can be a part of it. They must at least be informed of any changes I am there to implement, and I ask for their suggestions. Second, I will not take anything away from anyone. If this has to be done, the person who employed me must take that responsibility. I will not be viewed as an "enemy"; this will defeat my purpose. Therefore, I never had any problems working with people when I was brought in to change something that needed to be changed.

The very fact that the visiting nurse director had contacted my boss behind my back and asked her to visit so she could complain about me supported what I had seen clearly in the short time I was there. She had fully expected to encounter a young nurse, someone to whom the nursing director could dictate how she would implement the project. The director of the college was glad he had hired someone who knew how to do the project and work with people as well.

It was a great program, and all seventy-five students graduated at the end of the year. I had kept a scrapbook with many pictures recording various activities during the course. I presented this to the director of the college, and he was impressed that I had taken the time to prepare a pictorial record of the project. I met all the goals of the project, and the students enjoyed the courses as well.

The students were very pleased with the content of the classes and their teachers. Several of the women had dropped out of high school but had been able to earn a GED. One comment I heard often was, "If I'd had a teacher like you, I would have stayed in school." It is unfortunate, but most teachers prefer to teach fast learners. What they did not know was that my experience as a nurse gave me many of the tools I needed to reach them more effectively. Another factor was that they were older and had become more mature in their thinking and their ability to learn. What they were being taught was relevant to the way they earned their living, so it made more sense to them.

The women knew they were fortunate to have been chosen by their employer to receive this enrichment training, but they were sorry that this opportunity would not be available to others in the future. I asked their opinions about a lot of things related to the program and their knowledge of community needs. As a result of my discussions with them, I began to wonder if there were some way to continue the program. The college could not continue the program due to lack of funds.

By this time, Gary had bought a bass boat so we could fish in the freshwater lakes in the Houston area. Never in my wildest dreams did I think I would ever want to fish. I never even knew people who fished, except in the country, where most people had a small pond of their own. I viewed fishing and hunting as sports that men learned as boys from their fathers or grandfathers. Since Gary had been denied this privilege, what he knew he learned from studying books and talking to others who had learned at an early age about the pleasures of fishing. Now he had a pupil who knew absolutely nothing about the sport. But if it meant that we could be together, riding in the boat for fun, I was all for it. Fun was one thing that had been lacking in my life for many, many years.

Gary was very methodical in everything he did. Whether this came from his education or from some other source, I cannot say; however, he found in me fertile ground for his teaching. I had some of the same traits, which my father had taught me, but not quite as rigid as Gary's. From the beginning, he taught me what to do, but I would do it myself, which is pretty much the way I taught, too. I learned all about the different lures, lines, and bait. I had to tie the knot to perfection or I would lose my fish. I had my own tackle box stocked with everything I needed and knew how to use each item.

The Saturdays we would go fishing, I would pack a lunch for us, and we would start out just after breakfast. He learned early on that "I don't do early," so even though he talked a lot about being on the water at "first light," he would have had to go without me. We would troll around the edge of the lake. Bass boats have a shallow draft, and he would sit at the front, driving the trolling motor, while I sat in the back of the boat with my feet propped on the outboard motor. Everything was quiet until lunchtime, when he would anchor the boat under a bridge and we would sit and talk while eating lunch. Even now, I would give anything to be able to do that just one more time.

On one particular Saturday, the water on Lake Conroe was very rough, so Gary thought we should tie up under a bridge. Others were doing the same thing. You must remember that Gary was used to directing two sons on how to do things. Well, now he had me to direct. He would sit in the stern of the boat, guiding the motor, and I was to stand in the bow of the boat while casting the rope over the concrete supports under the bridge. I must tell you that the boat was moving vertically at least two feet up and down while I was standing up throwing the rope! I thought to myself, *What would my family and friends think if they could see me now?* It just didn't occur to me that I could fall out of the boat. Gary thought I could do anything his boys could do, and I came close. Remember, I told you early on that I like challenges; well, I had plenty!

After I had learned a lot about fishing, I usually caught more fish than Gary. At first I wanted to take them home, because I like fish. I said, "Chief catch fish, and Squaw clean and cook fish!" But later the fun was in the catching, and since Gary did not want to take the boat out of the water until the sun went down, it was too late for Squaw to "clean and cook fish." So Chief and Squaw released the fish and ate out!

On weekends when we didn't visit the lake with the boat, we went to the coast to fish in saltwater, which is a whole different way of fishing. Our favorite thing was to go to Galveston and fish from the jetties that protruded into the bay leading to the fifty-mile ship channel to the docks in Houston. The jetties extended into the water for about a fourth of a mile, and they regulated the currents and protected the bay water for the ships entering the ship channel. The jetties are about as wide as a driveway and are made of huge blocks of granite mined in Texas. There were all kinds of people fishing on the jetties. I used to say there were Mexicans, Vietnamese, blacks, poor whites, and the Davenports. It was really fun to be there, having conversations with all kinds of people whose one interest at the time was catching fish. "How ya' doing?" I might ask, and then I would learn what species of fish was running and what type of bait was successful. We really enjoyed sitting on the huge stones in the heat of the day with the coastal breezes cooling us off. Everyone is a friend just like you! Near the jetty that we went to most of the time, a woman used to come and sell tamales out of the back of her truck. That would be our lunch for the day.

One year, shortly after I went to Houston, we went to the jetty when the flounder were running. I had caught a number of fish, and Gary asked if I was ready to leave. I told him I would leave when I had six more flounder. In no time flat, I had six more flounder! Now that is really fun! But I'm sorry to say that by the time we left Houston the flounder had thinned out so much that we could not catch them like we had years earlier.

While I'm talking about Galveston, I would be amiss if I did not tell you about the ferry boat. The Galveston ferry is part of the Texas highway system, and it runs from Galveston across the bay to the Bolivar peninsula, where there are beaches. It is a free trip, and whenever visitors come to Houston, they always want to ride the ferry across the bay and back. It's a real experience. Teenagers ride the ferry across to go to the beach and have drinking parties, and some fall asleep on the benches as the boat returns to Galveston. You also have a number of those who have been fishing off the jetties, and you can imagine what they look like after fishing all day.

Up the Bolivar peninsula is a place called Rollover Pass. At this point, the water from the ocean runs through the pass into the intercoastal waterway. You'll see the same mixed mass of humanity you see fishing on the jetties on both sides of Rollover Pass. The difference is that the people come often at night with trucks, campers, and the like to spend the night either fishing or sleeping to get an early start the next morning. We fished from the banks but didn't go there very often. All along the coast in Texas are just so many wonderful places to fish.

Remember, early on, Gary and I were overwhelmed by the way Texas people lived. It was such a contrast to the way it was in South Carolina. The whole purpose of the work week was planning for the next weekend. After noon on Friday, it was impossible to find anyone in a business office, except the person answering the phone—and sometimes that person, too, had already left.

Since I was working that year with the community college, we decided we would do as Ruby had predicted: take a course in Spanish. We chose conversational Spanish, and if you know about that, it's all memory work. There was no way I was able to memorize at this point in my life. The teacher was a pharmacist from Cuba. The first night, I told Gary, "I can't tell when she changes from Spanish to English, her accent is so heavy," and she had been in the United States for about twenty years.

One assignment was to find pictures of clothing and paste or tape them to a sheet of paper. I carefully found the pictures and attached them to the paper with tape. The teacher would hold one up and ask the name of a certain piece of clothing. When she got to my pictures, they were all stuck together, and I realized I had used double-sided tape. I laugh a lot anyway, but as I watched her trying to separate the sheets of paper, I almost rolled out of my seat. Of course, Gary did not know why I was laughing so hard. The teacher said, "I don't know what's wrong with these sheets; I can't seem to get them apart." Well, that made it funnier than ever. Gary was so serious in class, but not me; I have been going to school all my adult life, and I go because I just enjoy learning so much. When I told him about the tape, he laughed, but not like I did. I wish you could have been there; it was really funny to see that teacher working so hard to pull the papers apart. We stayed in the class all semester, but we withdrew in good standing before the exam. Gary was ready to take the exam, but I wasn't. Since I already have a master's degree, any other learning is just fun. Wait until you read about our other experience.

Gary always worked very hard at his job and was very serious about doing everything just right. But during the first year of our marriage, he worked even harder, because he was in a new type of job. He was very happy playing with me; neither of us had ever played before. After all the hurts each of us had experienced, it was such a blessing to enjoy life again. We were pleased and excited that he was chosen for the President's Circle by Westinghouse Corporation. This meant that he was one of the best salesmen in all of Westinghouse. As a reward, we were flown to Pittsburgh for a weekend, where we stayed in an upscale hotel and were wined and dined. I was given a gold bracelet with a charm on it with my initials on one side and the President's Circle logo on the other side. I enjoy wearing it. He was given a beautiful gold watch; however, he put it in a drawer and never did wear it. He had a cheaper Timex that he liked better. I think the gold one was a bit too flashy for his taste. Notice I had no trouble wearing my bracelet!

# Davenport Home Assistants

## 1981-1983

All this time, I was still toying with the idea that I wanted to start a business; the home health students I had in my class wanted me to continue to teach so others could take the course. When we went fishing, I did some of my best thinking and planning. I visited the Chamber of Commerce to see if they thought this type of business was possible based on what was already available in the city. Their opinion was very positive; personal services, such as the type I envisioned, were now in demand and would be more so in the future.

My plan at that time was to teach a class and then place them in jobs. I would not have any licensed personnel, only the homemaker/health aide type. Their duties would be about the same as what they were doing with a volunteer health agency. They would work five days a week or live in with elderly people. These people would not work for me; rather, my business would recruit people, check references, and evaluate their performance. The employer would contact me, and I would evaluate the situation and then match an applicant with the job. The employer would have a meeting with the person, and it would be up to him or her whether to hire or not. I would charge a fee for that service.

My last contact was with the State Department of Education in Texas to get their endorsement and also to get their ideas on the teaching part of the plan. This would have been the procedure if I were doing it in South Carolina. The person I talked to liked my written plan and thought I had done a good job putting it on paper. Two things really surprised me. They did not want me to charge to train the people and then charge the employers as well. What really floored me was her saying, "You should have just gone ahead and done it. It would have been years before we even found out about it, and when we did, we could have evaluated the situation then."

The professional agencies use pretty much the same technique, but they do not train. However, in my plan, the placement fee is nowhere near what professionals get, and with the training and the placement fee, I would be able to generate enough money to keep the business going.

I determined that there was no need for me to work so hard and teach classes when there were experienced people walking the street that I could place in the kind of jobs I envisioned. I found an office in an area everyone was familiar with, bought some office furniture, put some ads in the paper, and got started. The phone started ringing immediately. I had two lines but saw right away that I would need a secretary to keep up with the calls.

Soon I was handling all kinds of help, and the business was growing. One problem was the time it took to counsel a family member about the needs of the patient. I simply could not charge what the conference really cost me in time, as well as the knowledge I was using to place one person.

It has been said that no house is big enough for two women, and that goes double when it's two older women. One day, a nice young man called me and suggested, "Mrs. Davenport, there are so many older women living alone. Why can't we put two of them together to share in the cost of daily living and provide companionship for each other?" Well, I almost laughed in his face, but I was very professional when I explained that that simply would not work. I had had a woman who tried to live with another woman who was a lot older, and when the younger woman went to stay with her, the older woman would not even give her a place to put her clothes. That's a simple and mild explanation; some are a lot worse. Women are so possessive of their homes; that's their domain. Another woman doesn't stand a chance, unless they are sisters and can freely argue with each other. Mothers with daughters are even worse. By the way, this is not new!

The business continued to grow, and at one point I had five people working for me. But it did not take me long to realize I did not want to continue to work this hard, so I decided to sell the business. I put an ad in the paper and promptly received several calls. Over a period of weeks, I continued to talk to people about my business. One woman was very interested, took a lot of my time, and gave me some money to assure me that she was serious. She wanted to wait about two months before she made up her mind. When the time came, however, she decided she no longer wanted the business.

The next person was the owner of a home health agency, and he came over to talk to me and assured me that he was very serious. His idea was to take over my business, and I would be his employee, which suited me fine; it was the responsibility that was taking a toll on my playtime. We discussed everything, and he was very pleased with the price I was asking. We talked for hours and had everything pretty much all worked out. The following Sunday, I went to the office and spent about five hours writing down everything he would need to operate the business pretty much the way I did. That was what he wanted. I felt very good about it, and the thought of working for someone else was a relief to me after all I had been through getting my business off the ground. He gave me his card and explained where he would be when I was ready to close the deal. I felt pleased as I placed all the papers into a manila envelope and dropped it in the mail.

Imagine my surprise when the envelope was returned to me! It was marked "unclaimed" and had not been opened. I called the number on the card the man had given me, and the phone had been discontinued. Would you believe I never heard from him again? Welcome to Houston!

I sat at my desk and prayed, "Okay, God, you know I don't want to be burdened with this business at my age, but if you want me to keep it, I'll do the best I can. Please don't forget this isn't what I want, but I have to assume this is what you want for me at this time. I'm okay with that. You have guided me in the past, and I have no reason to think you won't continue to be with me." At that point, I gave up trying to sell Davenport Home Assistants.

For the next year, I kept plugging away and gave it everything I had, and the business moved forward. All of a sudden, the phone just didn't ring. It was like someone had cut the cord. The paper had been filled with news about the slow economy in New England and other parts of the country, and now it had hit Houston. My first thought was, *Now I'll never be able to sell my business, and I'll have to let a couple of people go.* I had already fired one woman; she had just gone through a divorce and had not worked in quite some time. One of the other girls had begged me to hire her because of this, so I felt I should help her. Bad move; she was a problem from the beginning. Every week, just before we closed on Friday, she would drop something on me that would ruin my weekend. Finally, I had to fire her, and I never saw her again.

One day, I was sitting at my desk and received a phone call from a woman who said, "I am Jane Brown, from a company in California, and we would like to buy your business!"

I almost fell over but said, "Do you know what kind of business I have?"

"Yes, we know all about you."

I just couldn't believe it, and, after my earlier experiences, I didn't know what to expect. She told me the company she worked for was moving into Houston and wanted to buy up its competitors. She asked my price, and I gave her the same one I had quoted before. I explained I had recently had surgery, which was true, and I was ready to give up the business. She said she would get back to me after she discussed the price with her superiors.

In about a week, she called me back to say the price was right, and they would follow through with the sale. We discussed my employees: two they would keep, and one part-time person did not need to work; she was my friend, and she would not stay. Then we discussed the furniture, records, and other things pertinent to the sale. She always flew to do her work, and we set a date when she would fly into Houston to an airport near my home. I was not excited; I was afraid this was just another big-city deal that would fail like the last two. So you could say I held my breath!

This was winter, and at about ten o'clock I received a call that Dallas was snowed in and they could not fly out. She would be in touch. All of us just sighed and went on with the work. At about noon, she called to say the runways had been cleared; she was on her way and would be at my office in about two hours. She was there just as she said. She handed me a check, we set a date to turn it over to her company, and in forty-five minutes she was gone. What an easy sale! God knew exactly what he was doing, and he was with me just like he had always been.

Now that my business was sold, I told myself I would not get into anything like that again. However, I have to admit that if I had been younger, I would have enjoyed providing services to older people. The demand is still there today.

In the spring we had a large fishing show in the arena part of the Astrodome complex. Gary and I decided we would go to see what was new. We did not stay together; I was looking at lures, and he was looking at something else. I had always liked a Rapala lure, so I was talking to a man about what I thought were positive aspects of the lure when he said, "Where in South Carolina are you from?"

I said, "Where do you think I'm from?"

He answered, "Well, you don't talk like the mountain area, and you certainly don't talk like the coastal area, so I'd guess you're from the midlands!"

"You're right!" I told him. We really took off in a long conversation about geography and fishing. There were two other incidents in Houston when people identified my home by my speech.

At this same show, we saw someone trying to sell time shares in vacation homes. After he did his pitch to Gary and me, I looked through his catalog and saw Deercreek, on the coast of South Carolina. I told Gary, "I have one of those on the coast of South Carolina." I had completely forgotten about it. It was in the seventies when the concept of time shares first came to South Carolina. Earle and I saw the ads and went to Surfside Beach just to look. I ended up buying two weeks, Memorial Day week and Thanksgiving week. Never in my wildest dreams did I think I would ever leave South Carolina, but in the back of my mind was the idea that I could at least get away from home two weeks out of the year. With this purchase came a membership in Resorts Condominium International, which permitted me to make exchanges wherever these home communities were located. This purchase would end up being very special for Gary and me.

Our pastor at First United Methodist Church in Houston took groups to Israel about twice a year. We decided we would like to go with him on his next trip. At the time, there was a lot of unrest in Israel, but he assured us we had nothing to fear, so off we went. We flew into Amman, Jordan, and spent the night. The next day, we boarded the Jordanian bus and went to the border with Israel, where we had to walk through a customs building; on the other side, we boarded an Israeli bus for our tour. It was when I was putting the pictures into albums that I noticed all the guns on the hill, pointed at the customs building, which I'm sure would have been blown up had any of us posed a big threat.

What always comes as a surprise to people when they visit Israel is how small it is. I remind them that people walked or rode donkeys wherever they went. Perhaps you've noticed this, too; everyone who goes wants to see the places we know from the Bible, so it doesn't take very long to see all the places Jesus travelled. The trip was not exactly what we had hoped for, but since it was our first trip together, it was an exciting experience. Our nationally known Pastor was a group person, meaning a person who needs large groups to speak to, but no good at one on one conversation. Gary really wanted to get to know him personally, but the Pastor never saw anyone individually. Most of the time he was asleep on the back seat of the tour bus.

We have three albums filled with pictures from that trip. Gary always kept a log of the pictures he took, but not everyone does that. After we had been home for a while, a woman called Gary and told him she had lots of pictures that were all filled with rocks, and she had no idea where they had been taken or what they were. She came to see his pictures to try to identify hers, but I don't think she was very successful.

You already know how overwhelmed we were with Texas; everything was so new and different. We did a condo swap and took a week in Tyler, Texas. One morning, after a cool front had passed through, we walked out of the condo, and the sky was the bluest I had ever seen. The Tyler courthouse had a silver dome and was silhouetted against the blue sky. Miss Justice was standing with her scales at the top of the dome, and we thought it was just gorgeous. Gary, who always had his camera, took a picture of the courthouse and the dome. Then I had a thought: why not photograph all the county courthouses in Texas? At that point in time, I had no idea what I was suggesting. But we thought that would give us a chance to really see all of the state. I learned later that there were 254 counties in Texas. Thus began a four-year odyssey.

# Making A Way

## 1982-1986

You have to remember that I did not have a job, so I just made a job for myself. I would plan a trip to an area and, if possible, get a time share and spend the week going to the various counties. Ray Miller wrote several books, each one about an area of Texas. We bought the books, and as we drove from town to town, I would read all about where we were going. Once we were there, I would tell Gary exactly what shots I wanted. I always wanted a full front and rear, the dome, and the entrance. I would strike up a conversation with anyone I could find and get them to tell me something about their county building. People everywhere were interested in what we were doing and were proud to tell us stories about the building and some of the things that had happened there. While Gary was doing the photographs, I would walk around outside, looking for things I felt were significant to the people in that particular county. Almost every weekend, we spent the whole time "courthousing," as we called it. The time share I had bought in South Carolina was exchanged for one in an area we needed to visit to take photographs. We had such a wonderful time. But by the time the four years were over, we were ready to do something else. As I sit here and write about it, I am left with the feeling that we really did accomplish something very meaningful. I made a job for myself since I was now retired and handled every photograph and mounted two thousand of them into five albums. While Gary was taking photos, I made notes as I observed the grounds and monuments or markers of all types, and I wrote about what I had observed. We photographed old jails and county markers as well.

I was in touch with the Texas Historical Commission, which was very interested in our project. It became known as the Red and Emily Davenport Collection and is in the library at Baylor University in Waco, Texas. We were on TV in Houston, and the Houston *Chronicle* did a five-page spread about us and our project. Before we left Houston, I talked to the librarian, and she told me that two of the Texas courthouses had burned and our photographs would aid in their rebuilding. We were told at the time that our work was the best they had of all the courthouses as they were at that time. Baylor gave us a lovely plaque for our donation.

Perhaps you aren't familiar with the Elderhostel programs. I first heard about the organization from some retired public school teachers. The organization is based in Boston, Massachusetts. Any educational entity can apply to put on a program that is specifically for older adults. After a program has been approved, it is published in a newsletter. Members look at the programs and decide where they would like to go and what they would like to study and then make their application. During the eighties, the programs in the United States started on Sunday afternoon and ended at Saturday noon. There were classes every day, and the instructors were outstanding— all of this for a very low fee. Gary and I attended twenty of these programs together, and I have been to two since he passed away. Many changes have taken place in the last few years, but I still think it is a wonderful experience that enables you to meet other people like yourself who like to travel and learn.

After I had been in Houston for about five years, I learned about the Women's Institute, which had been established to give affluent, nonworking wives the chance to expand their knowledge. I read about the Institute in the paper and decided it was a school I would like to attend. The courses were noncredit but taught by instructors from the University of Houston or Rice University. I applied and was accepted. I did not know any of the others attending, but I learned so much. No tests—just what I enjoy, fun learning.

During this time, along with dancing and fishing and studying, we were also travelling. Our first trip was a survey of Europe, where we visited seven countries. The idea was just to get an overview of the different countries and then take a trip to a specific country to get more in-depth information. We went to England, Scotland, and Wales. Later we went to Ireland. Our tour was the first tour to go into Northern Ireland in quite some time, because of the political unrest there. I was wearing a University of South Carolina sweatshirt as we walked into a restaurant. A young man came over to me and asked, "Did you go to USC?"

I replied, "Yes, I sure did."

"So did I," he said. I thought that was pretty amazing. We spent a few minutes talking about the school and South Carolina. It was quite a thrill.

One year, Gary and I went to Saudi Arabia for Christmas with Katy and her family. We were there for three weeks, and it was a great trip. I found it interesting to see Christmas decorations in this Muslim country.

After studying the historical geography of Spain at the Women's Institute, I wanted to go to Spain. The ten-day trip included Spain, Portugal, and Morocco. It was ten days neither of us would ever forget. The tour started in Spain, and it was most interesting to see the places I had studied.

We went to Gibraltar, which is just a small piece of land of 2.5 square miles, consisting mostly of a rocky hill. It is a British crown colony, where there are a port and a naval base overlooking the Strait of Gibraltar. We crossed over the strait, passed into Morocco, and motored on to a very nice hotel for the night. We were told that some on the tour wanted to visit the city's casino. I was tired and not at all interested in a casino, but Gary said he would like to go, so I encouraged him. The bus left the hotel, and at midnight he was still not back from the casino. Time passed, and still no Gary. I called the desk and was told the bus had returned quite some time ago. I was very concerned, plus I wanted to go to sleep; I'm sort of a sleepyhead anyway. It was almost 3:00 AM when Gary walked in the door.

I don't know which of us was in worse condition. It seems that the bus driver had counted heads as he left the hotel, and the passengers were told to return to the drop-off point at 10:30 PM. Most of the people didn't want to stay long, so they were back at the bus early. The driver counted heads and was sure he had the same count as before, so he returned to the hotel. But of course he was wrong. Gary had been left at the casino, and he had no idea where he was staying. He, like all tour passengers, had just followed the tour director when he took us into the hotel. I was frantic at the hotel, but it was nothing like how frantic Gary was at the casino; he had no idea where we were staying and couldn't think of the name of the tour company. (We had taken a number of tours by this time, and they all had different names.) I had all the paperwork; all he had was his passport. Of course he knew *who* he was, but he didn't know *where* he was.

Someone contacted the manager, and the questioning went on. The city of Marrakesh is large and has a number of hotels that house tour groups. It just so happened that the manager had cashed a check for a women he thought had come in at the time our group did. After many phone calls, he was able to locate our tour. The casino manager drove Gary to our hotel. He was so glad to see me. He had never been comfortable travelling in foreign countries, and this was probably the first time in his adult life that he did not have everything under control.

The next day, we visited an outlying area of the city, where many poor people lived. We went into their "homes," where they had dirt floors and no running water or other conveniences found in modern countries. We saw what they were cooking and talked to the woman who lived in the first one we entered. It was obvious that she knew we were coming, and this was sort of a demonstration for us, I think. It is my guess that the woman and others were paid to give us a peek at the way they lived; I hope so.

Later, I think it was the same day but I'm not sure, I began to feel nauseated, and when we went to supper, I did not want to eat.

The tour director told the waiter to bring me rice soup and said it would fix me in a hurry. What they called rice soup was the water drained off the rice after it was boiled. In college, we starched our clothes with it. So I ate my rice soup and nothing else for supper. But in the morning, I was ready to get going again. I have always done well physically on trips; this problem was my first, and I did not have anymore problems, not then! But I can assure you, we were very glad to get back home, and we did not do anymore tours.

By this time, we were beginning to think of Gary's retirement and all that would entail for us. First of all, we loved living in Texas, as you know, but did we want to stay there throughout retirement? Gary would have been happy to stay in Texas, but I wanted to be closer to the East Coast for my family and the ease of travel. Both of us loved to drive, but we wanted to be near an airport as well. You think of all these things and write them down just to get started, but then when you make up your mind, half of these desires might have changed or even disappeared.

I did not want to deal with a large city as we grew older. The traffic was terrible in Houston, and shopping for clothing was a real disappointment to me. In fact, I would wait until I visited Columbia to buy clothes. In a large city, the stores are more specialized, and that means travelling for miles to buy shoes one place, dresses another place, and specialty items somewhere else. Buying clothes would fill one whole day. Shopping for groceries was not a problem.

We were driving over twenty miles to church each Sunday, and that distance made it difficult for us to participate in the church's other activities. I felt that I would like to live in an area where I could drive to see my children and grandchildren. Gary wanted to be near a golf course so he could play often. I wondered why, since we lived on the sixteenth fairway in Houston and he'd played just three times. Remember, that was one thing he'd planned to do when he was transferred to Houston. But after he had me with him, somehow he didn't really want to play golf anymore. He wanted me to take golf lessons twice, and though I was getting the hang of it, we never played together, which was probably a good thing.

I bought a number of books on retirement do's and don'ts and what to look for. What type of home would you live in? How big? What about a church? Were there intellectual pursuits? And, most of all, was there good healthcare? How about the weather? That was a big one; Gary had lived about twenty years in the North, so he knew he didn't want to live anyplace where there was snow and/or ice. We wanted an airport nearby, and the discussions went on and on.

It was about this time that computers were being talked about, and there were a number of people, mostly young people, who had home computers. We did not have the Internet available yet. But Gary liked to be first in getting everything, so we bought a computer made by AT&T. He never touched it; he wanted it for me. If I would get frustrated, he would sit by me and say, "Why don't you do this or that?" But he never would touch it. It was about this time that he wanted us to take a basic course in computers at the community college. So I agreed to make all the arrangements.

We showed up for the class, and the room was set up in a strange formation. For this class, I guess it was all right. The computers were arranged along the window wall and across the back wall. We went toward the windows, and Gary wanted me ahead of him, so he pulled out the chair for the first machine, which put me in the corner. Then he sat next to me. We had a good teacher, and the instructions were clear, especially since we were all green beginners.

In all my years of schooling, I had few men in my classes. So I was used to talking to the people around me, and as we learned new things, we would share with one another. Gary was different. If he knew something I didn't know, he would not share with me; rather, he would smile and look like a kid who had been given candy—and no, I could not have any. I tried to move to another computer, but he wanted me to stay by him. This went on for the whole semester, and I really didn't care whether I learned anything or not. Remember, I am the happy student, but I was not a happy student in this class. Gary never did touch the computer at home. Sometimes he would ask me to type something for him, and I would. This competition thing was something I had never seen before, so I lost interest in the class.

The night of the final exam, Gary was late getting home, and when we arrived at the class, another male student was sitting at my computer. So I had to go to one in the back of the room. Well, that was the last straw, and I really didn't care whether I even passed or not. Our grades were mailed to us, and when they arrived, Gary had an A and I had a B. He was very upset that I did not have an A. He said, "You know more about the computer than I do; you should have had an A."

I refused to talk about it. But I did say, "I will never—get this, never, ever—take another class with you. I was not in competition with you; I didn't care whether I received a grade or not. My classes at this point in my life are for fun, pure and simple. This one was not a fun class." I think he really felt bad that I had not received an A. We never took another class together.

The retirement discussion took a lot of time, and we finally ruled out many things. Gary mentioned Greenville, South Carolina, but he had been gone for so long that he had no friends there. His mind really changed when I told him that in the past I had had to cancel programs in Greenville due to the icy weather. He suggested Columbia, but I ruled that out because my first husband was still living there. Knowing Earle as well as I did, I felt it would not be a good thing for me to move back there at this particular time. He was living alone in a duplex. Finally, we settled on Florida, more specifically, central Florida. This fulfilled one of our plans since Gary had a son in Dothan, Alabama, and I had a daughter in Naples, Florida. Both our children were about three to four hours driving time away, but in opposite directions.

We made several trips to Florida to look for a place to retire. One location appealed to me, especially when I first saw it. It was October, and fall was in the air. The sun was shining brightly, a light breeze was blowing, and it reminded me of South Carolina. The development was Quail Run, located in the rolling hills, with lots of beautiful large oak trees filled with moss. The weather was not hot, and we learned later that the winters were mild and that there were about two freezes each year.

When we went to our motel room, we were very happy about Quail Run. Gary had lived most of his life in a city, so being in what was referred to as a semirural area would be new to him. I made it very plain that he, not I, must make the final decision about the place. He had never lived in a rural area. I am happy anywhere and I knew I would be happy there. The next morning, he had made his decision: he wanted us to move there. There were several golf courses nearby, as well as a freshwater lake, and the Gulf was only seventeen miles away.

The next day, we returned to Quail Run. We picked a lot, which was about a third of an acre. We picked a house plan and did all the other things that needed to be done to transform this idea into reality. Making the decision as to *where* was the hard part.

Since the church we attended in Houston was so far away, I started looking for a closer one where I might attend Bible studies or have some other religious activity during the week. A few blocks from where we lived was a Bible church. I found out they had a weekly Bible study, with classes for children as well. On my own, I went one Thursday, and I was impressed with their program. So I continued to attend.

Each week, Gary and I went square dancing with three couples who were our friends. We four wives also went to lunch once a week, and one week, I invited them to come to the Bible study with me before we went to lunch. One by one, over a period of time, they joined me. Most of the women at the Bible study were young, first-time mothers, and they enjoyed us older women, especially when we told them that this rough time with a small baby would be over in no time.

On one of our many trips from Florida, when we were returning to Houston from Atlanta, I was sitting in the middle seat as always. I have flown many times, and I know some people do not want to be disturbed by a stranger, so I have always carried a book to read. On this trip, I had my book out before the plane took off.

A middle-aged woman was sitting by the window. After a few minutes she said to me, "Do you live in Houston?"

I replied, "Yes, I do. Do you?"

Thus a conversation was started, so it continued. She answered, "No, but I will be. I'm on my way to Houston to be married!"

My answer was, "I did the same thing seven years ago." Well, there was no stopping us now! I was familiar with the Houston area because of my business, so I asked, "In what area will you be living?"

She could not tell me the area, but she gave me the address so I could look it up when I arrived home. She wanted my phone number, which I gave her, and I told her to call me and I would show her around the city. She did not know anyone in Houston except her intended husband, whom she had known since grammar school. Later, I sent them a card wishing them well for their wedding.

Some weeks passed, and I thought I would not hear from her again, but that did not happen. She got in touch with me, and I visited her home and learned that she actually lived closer to me than any of my other friends. She met all my friends and joined us at the Bible study and lunch each week. But due to some residual effects from polio when she was young, she could not dance with us.

Her name was Fran, and we have been friends for years. From her first day in Houston, she had friends because she spoke to me on the plane. I'm sure she really wanted to tell me how blessed and happy she was to be starting a new life, and she found someone who could identify exactly with the way she felt. You never know who God will put in your path. Do as Gary always told me: "Be alert!"

The downturn in the economy was still going on in 1988, so we expected to have some difficulty selling our house in Houston. Of course, the price had gone down, but we knew God was with us and that it would sell. We had a patio home with zero lot-line construction on the sixteenth fairway in Quail Valley, a very nice place to live. At the end of our street were several condos, and very soon a couple who lived in one of the condos wanted to buy our house. They were familiar with the neighborhood, so it was not necessary to "sell" the house after they saw it. One wall in the living/dining room had been paneled a dark brown when the house was built. I had it painted turquoise to go with my furniture. They had a couch to put against that wall, and she was ecstatic about the color choice. You never really know what will appeal to other people when they are house shopping.

Now that we'd sold our house, the buyers wanted it as soon as possible, so it was necessary for us to make some arrangements to move. We found a corporate apartment and were allowed to bring some of our furniture; the rest was put into storage until we moved to Florida. I started packing with three different stacks. One stack went to the apartment, one was to go to storage, and the other we would move ourselves. By this time I was pretty good at packing.

The day we moved into the apartment, a hurricane came through. The forecast called for it to hit Houston, but it moved more south before making landfall. But the rain came down in torrents, with lots of wind. The apartment was up a flight of steps, and you had to make a sharp turn at the top to get into the living room. I really felt sorry for the movers, but they did a good job, and none of the furniture got wet. We were there for six months.

During the time we were living there, I continued to do what has to be done when a family moves out of state. In the summer of that year, 1988, Gary sold the bass boat and bought a deep V-hull boat so we could take it into the saltwater at Galveston. It would be just right for going into the coves along the Florida coast as well. We took it out about three times before we moved. It was very heavy, so we just went to the jetties like we always did and enjoyed it so much. Gary said that the fun of a boat was to own it.

# Retirement in Florida

## 1989-1998

The weather in Houston was bad when we left for Florida. Gary drove our van and towed the boat, and I drove the car. We moved into our new house on April 3, 1989. The next day was my birthday. We had a good trip, but we were happy the move was over. I had found dry storage for the boat, and some things we had bought earlier were all in place in the house.

When people think of Florida, they think of palm trees; but in central Florida, where our house was located, we had lovely large oaks with moss in them. We had a spacious lot with a curved driveway and beautiful oaks in our backyard. There were not but a few houses there when we moved in, but the place kept growing. It was so peaceful, not at all like driving miles and miles in very heavy traffic like it was in Houston. I'm sure Gary missed his buddies from work, but he never said he did.

We met a couple who liked to square dance, and we went dancing one night, but most of the people were older, and I'm afraid it wasn't as lively as our Texas dancing. Gary said he no longer wanted to dance; he didn't like to dance like they did.

The developer had not made a phone list or prepared the information people needed when they moved into Quail Run. I went from house to house getting phone numbers, addresses, and other information to put together lists for everyone. When new people moved in, I would take the list and visit them, giving them information about the county services and answering questions about area resources. We had been living there for about a year before I started this, so we were very familiar with the area.

Some days were so beautiful, sunny, and warm, and I would suggest taking the boat out. But he always had an excuse. He might say, "I don't think *you* want to go today, because it's a bit windy." He never said *he* didn't want to go. Then he decided perhaps if the boat had a canvas top over it to protect us from the sun it would be better and we would enjoy it more. So he proceeded to take the boat to a canvas place so they could design a top for it. There were fold-down seats in the boat, so with a top over us, we could fish and float all day; the breeze from the water would keep us cool. But I never even got into the boat or fished while we lived in Florida.

Gary and I took the AARP 55 Alive driving course so we could get a reduced rate on our car insurance. After we took the course, we decided we would like to teach it since both of us were good drivers with clean driving records. Both of us became certified instructors, and we taught six classes each year for three years. At the instructors' training sessions, if there were handouts, each of us wanted our own paper. It was sort of funny that the other couples shared theirs but we did not share ours. I think there were two reasons. One, each of us was an only child. Two, we didn't feel we could trust anyone else to handle something we were responsible for. Gary and I had many of the same characteristics that I always attributed to the fact that we were reared alone.

We joined the United Methodist church in Inverness after visiting a number of different churches. We were members for three years. However, I felt something wasn't right at that church. Sometimes you just feel something isn't right, but you really don't know what it is. I knew that each Sunday after church I was just so angry, and that is not the way one should feel after worship. I told Gary I was going to leave that church, which was something I would never do without just cause, even if it was just feelings. I suggested that he could continue to go there, but he chose to do whatever I did.

My daughter Ann lived in Naples, Florida, and when she came to visit us, she suggested that we visit the Episcopal church in Dunnellon, where she went on her visits. It was closer but in the opposite direction. We did visit, and we liked it the first Sunday, and we stayed there until our lives changed again. While I was there, I was elected president of the Daughters of the King.

Our little community continued to grow, and two of the women came to see me and asked me to get some things started at our clubhouse. I agreed if they would help me. Here, again, just like in the years before, people were looking for someone to do something nobody else would do. I always liked the challenge to see if I could do it. First, I organized the community and started a homeowners' group that would meet each month. So many people had brought books there and we started a library. I set up the cards and folders for checking out the books. I started a Bible study and later turned it over to a man who wanted very much to teach it.

Things were moving along really well, but the last and most important thing I started was a ladies' group. We had two single women in our community, and I urged them to take it over, which they did. This was the beginning of getting speakers and having some other very interesting programs. By this time, I was writing a column for our weekly county newspaper.

I thought it was so much fun to get our development organized, and the residents were so happy that things had moved along so well. We had a lovely, large swimming pool that everyone enjoyed, and because each person was so helpful and wanted to be involved, it was easy to get things accomplished. I was very satisfied that I had faced the challenge and conquered it.

Both Gary and I were on some maintenance medications, which we had been taking for a number of years. I had found a doctor I liked very much, and I felt I could trust him to care for us. One morning, Gary told me he had an appointment to see our doctor to have his prescriptions renewed. I was not aware that he had made the appointment, so I had a conflict. We always went everywhere together, so I was surprised that he had made the appointment and I did not know about it. He assured me that he did not need for me to go with him since he was just getting prescriptions. He said he had a few questions he wanted to ask the doctor. I suggested that he write them down, because patients seem to forget questions they want to ask the doctor and think of them as soon as they get back home. He assured me he had written them down.

When he returned home, my first question was, "How was your visit to the doctor?"

He was sort of evasive when he said, "I have to have an upper GI." I was very surprised, but that was all I got, and the test had been scheduled. I asked why the doctor had ordered that test. He said he didn't know. In the next few minutes, he went out to his shop in the garage, and I could hear him tinkering with his tools, which he loved to do.

I walked into the bedroom, and found the list he had taken to the doctor on top of the chest of drawers. I picked it up and read it, and my heart just sank. Everything he had listed was a symptom of cancer! Typical of his personality, he had never said a word to me. He knew himself what it meant, I'm sure, and he didn't want to tell me.

Both of us were strong type-A personalities, and I knew that on many occasions we had gone for the Mylanta or the Tums at the same time. There was nothing more than that. However, then I remembered several occasions when he came home from work in the evening looking very pale and extremely tired. Once I said, "Well, you might make it until your retirement, but I'm not sure I will." I had been busy all day packing and getting everything ready for our move. He said he'd had a very busy day, so that was that.

Even as sure as I was of his diagnosis, we did not discuss the upcoming test. But, like most women, I pondered it in my heart. I don't mind confessing that I couldn't help but constantly remember everything in the past that hadn't meant anything at the time but now had a distinct meaning. After being a registered nurse for forty-five years, I couldn't erase the things going through my brain day and night.

Finally, the day came for his upper GI test. I went with him, and we waited for the report. The films showed an abnormal appearance at the cardiac junction. This junction is where the esophagus empties into the stomach. We were not given a diagnosis then, but he was scheduled to have a CAT scan at the hospital in Ocala, about twenty-five miles from our house. We were not told anything yet, but he was referred to an oncologist, Dr. Anju Vasudevan, because the doctors knew what they were seeing with the upper GI; but a final diagnosis would not be given to us until the CAT scan was done. This test could present more detailed information, such as how big the tumor was, how involved it was, what the future indications of this diagnosis were, life expectancy, and so much more. Extensive lab work was being done as well.

When all this was done, we were presented with the findings. Gary had cancer, the type was adenocarcinoma. The onset was at the cardiac junction and is often referred to as a smoker's cancer. But there was more: the tumor had grown into the pancreas. The organs in this part of the body all lie against one another, so it's very easy for a tumor to grow from one organ to another. Adenocarcinoma is a slower-growing cancer, which explained a lot of things to me. Do not confuse Gary's cancer with pancreatic cancer, which has its onset in the pancreas. It is a fast-growing cancer with few treatments even now, in 2009.

It was at this time that we met Dr. Vasudevan. Dr. Anju was a little woman in stature but a giant in oncology. She was a native of India, as was her husband, who was a cardiologist. Both of them practiced medicine in Ocala, Florida. She was the center of our lives for six long years.

Next, Gary was referred to gastroenterologists so that that doctor could actually see the area of the tumor with the endoscope. He confirmed everything we already knew. But we were told that he had from six weeks to three months to live and that we should get our financial affairs in order. What a shock!

Gary would sit in the chair in the living room and I would sit on the floor at his feet as we reviewed all the wonderful times we'd had together during the last thirteen years. He had made up his mind that he was going to fight this disease to the bitter end. We spent many hours just grieving together. He did not want to die and leave me alone, and I had to think about what my life would be without him. But, being a nurse, I was determined that he would get the very best care I could provide to make it as easy for him as possible. The treatment went on for years and years, but each of us tried to make the very best of a bad situation. He was a firm believer in God and so was I, and we knew God would be there for us whatever we had to face.

Before treatment could begin, Dr. Anju had to determine whether the tumor in the pancreas was the same tumor that was in the esophagus or if it was a tumor of another type. This test required a needle biopsy. A radiologist would do the biopsy. He tried one afternoon but had no luck, but when we returned the next morning he was successful, and it was determined to be the same type. Now the treatment could begin.

The treatment would consist of radiation and chemotherapy. Dr. Brant was a radiation oncologist. He was from South Carolina, near my home, but was educated in Florida. He was very good and made us feel that Gary was receiving the very best of care. The radiation facility was nearer to us than the hospital, and we went there twice a week until the sixty treatments were completed.

The chemo was different. He had to go into the hospital for one week every six weeks until the lab reports reached a certain point. The chemo was given by continuous I.V. the whole time he was in the hospital. We met wonderful nurses on the oncology floor, so I guess you could say we were all in the same boat, but some patients were worse than others. There were beds in each room, and Dr. Anju wanted me to spend the night to save me the driving. But I went home every night, because I needed that time to rest my body and have some quiet time. Gary did not mind that I went home.

One of the things that amazed me was that Gary never complained, not once. He really wanted to get well. But even more than that, he did talk about how tired the radiation made him feel, but he was never sick at all while he was getting chemo. Patients who let their heads overrule their bodies seem to do well in dire situations like the ones he had to face. Dr. Anju proved over and over that she knew her medications well and that she knew how to manage her patients. Gary and I had put our lives into God's hands many years before, so whatever was going to happen to us, we knew we would be able to handle it with God's help.

After we received Gary's diagnosis, so many things became clearer to me. He had obviously been sick for a long time. No wonder on occasion he would look so bad when he came in from work. No wonder he didn't want to dance anymore, and, naturally, he did not want to take the boat out. The boat was extremely heavy, and he really was not able to handle it alone. He did not want to admit that he wasn't feeling well or disappoint me since I loved the boat. As much as he had always tried to please me, he thought it better just to make me think he was trying to protect me rather than to appear weak himself. The men who grew up in our generation felt that being sick or showing any sign of weakness was wrong. Their role as the sole breadwinner for the family meant it was their responsibility to always be strong, no matter what happened, so they could protect their families. This is the same reason, in most cases, the husband handled the money and insisted on driving the car. The overall impression we had when we were growing up was that a woman simply was not capable of doing these things. Gary's behavior was typical of men who grew up before the women's movement in the sixties, which changed everything.

During the first several years of Gary's illness, he felt pretty well, and we were able to continue to attend Elderhostels and take trips. Dr. Anju and I planned the trips together so as not to interfere with his treatments. Throughout his illness, I made it my "job" to keep our lives as normal as possible, and travelling was one thing we both enjoyed so much. We went all over each of the fifty states, visited seven provinces in Canada, and went to one place in Mexico. We had no pets, so it was easy to leave home for long periods of time.

After things settled down for us, the women in Quail Run were restless and wanted me to plan something for them. I asked them to give me some time to work on it. I had a great story in my mind, so I wrote a two-act play, *Holding On*. *Holding On* was about two couples who moved to Florida. The wife of one of the couples wanted to move, and we watched them going through the pros and cons before they actually made their decision. The other couple was more affluent. The husband was the typical CEO type; he made all the decisions and simply told his wife what they were going to do. The residents loved the play when they read it and wanted me to get it started at once. I volunteered to be the director after their prodding. We had all types of personalities in Quail Run, so it was easy for me to cast the characters. Then rehearsals started and went on for weeks. At the beginning, I told them of my experience in TV and what I wanted from them. I would make the decisions, and if there were other opinions, we would discuss them together. It was amazing that everyone memorized his or her part and got right into the characters. One couple wanted to get the props and other things that we needed; Gary had lots of musical tapes, and he would be in charge of the music; and I put together the programs since I had a computer. I scheduled one performance of the play for those who lived in Quail Run.

I had envisioned a fun thing to entertain the women, but it just became bigger and bigger. Finally, the night came for the dress rehearsal, and I was shocked, honestly, at how good it was. The characters were so true to life as the actors delivered their lines; I couldn't believe it.

What they didn't know was that I had used dialogue I had actually heard during my visits to the new people. What they said was typical not only of those who lived in Quail Run but of all those who move to Florida. I could predict the laughter, because everyone there could identify with the dialogue. The audience was actually seeing themselves, and that made the play successful.

After the performance, everyone was so pleased and wanted to put it on again. They told me that "so and so" wanted to see it, and someone wanted us to come to their development and put it on. By this time, and with Gary's illness, I was having muscle spasms in my back, and I realized I could not pursue their suggestions. Many pictures were taken, and the cast was just thrilled at what they had done. One couple gave us a party after the play, and a large picture of me as writer and director was on the front page of our county newspaper.

I told my friends that I had another story in my head and that I would try to get it written so we could do another play. But as time passed and my schedule became more complicated, I knew there was no way I would be able to write and direct another play, no matter how much I wanted to.

It became obvious that Gary would live beyond the predictions. He was not going to give up, and neither was I. He was monitored very closely, and this meant a trip to Ocala, twenty-five miles away, at least once a week and sometimes more. We would make it a day trip and always went to our favorite seafood place for lunch. He loved shrimp scampi, and I always had their shrimp salad. The waitresses recognized us we went so often. There were many, many other times that we just sat in our living room, crying together and reliving our meeting and the early years we spent together in Houston.

I have already told you how I got into sewing and making clothes for my three girls and myself. Then I made all my square dance dresses when we were in Houston. At this time, I really needed a new sewing machine, so we visited a shop in Ocala to look at their machines. The home computerized machines were fairly new, and this place sold them. Gary insisted that he wanted me to have a computerized machine, and at that time they were about $3,100. I insisted that I really didn't need one that expensive, but he was determined that I should have the best. So we carried one home. I took classes off and on for several months to learn to use all its features. It had discs for embroidery, monogramming, and other fun things. I put some kind of decoration on my T-shirts and monogrammed towels and pillowcases. I have to admit I thoroughly enjoyed that purchase.

But that wasn't enough: he wanted me to have a serger as well. I knew nothing about a serger, had never seen one, so I did not have much input. When I heard it was another $3,000, I said, "No way." I didn't think I would need it; I had sewn for years without one and had not done too badly. We left with a used one for $400, quite a difference. We were told that because a serger is harder to learn to use, most people take one home and never touch it again. Well, that wasn't for me. I went to the shop for more lessons and learned what a joy it was just to fly through hemming of any kind. That alone made it worth its cost.

Like everything else with Gary, there was more to this story than what you might think. His college degree was in industrial engineering, and his greatest joy was to hear machines running. He liked for me to sew so he could hear the machine. During his illness, I made slacks, dresses, blouses, and some other things I never wore so he could have the pleasure of "his" machines. It took me a while to realize what all this was about, but once I did there was always something I "wanted" to make.

In one way it happened slowly, and in another it seemed to happen so fast, but Gary became sicker and sicker. He was losing weight steadily, even though his diet was planned to maintain his weight and keep up his strength. Instead of wanting to be doing something all the time or going somewhere, he was now more comfortable sitting on our enclosed porch in the lounge chair. We had always had one bird feeder, because birds were everywhere in our backyard with the beautiful trees. I bought two more feeders to attract different kinds of birds. For the first time in his life, he watched the birds. We had two pairs of cardinals that stayed all year round and had their young in our backyard. If you saw the male or the female alone, you could look carefully and see the other bird nearby. One thrilling thing was the first day he saw the male bird take a seed and put it in the beak of the female bird. When his son came to visit, he was amazed that his father was so content watching the birds. When we are well and leading a busy life, earning a living and/or rearing a family, it's very easy to miss all the wonderful things in our environment that we never have time to see and appreciate.

Just before my seventy-fifth birthday in 1998, Gary wanted us to take a cruise to celebrate. We sailed out of Fort Lauderdale on a Saturday, and he was feeling better than he had been feeling for quite a while. During the night, he woke me up and told me he was freezing. I got up, found blankets in the closet, covered him, and noticed that he had a fever. The next morning he said he felt all right and wanted to take the tour of the small island that was our first stop. I never tried to stop him from doing what he felt he could do.

We went ashore and did the tour, but toward evening he was not feeling well at all. I had bought insurance when I got the tickets just in case he could not complete the trip. I reminded him of this, but he would not hear of cancelling. Then I suggested that he see the ship's doctor, but he said, "I'll wait until I can see Dr. Anju. She'll know what to do." I knew this would be our last trip, so I brought breakfast and lunch to him every day, but he insisted on dressing for dinner each night, where we sat with our new friends from Canada.

As soon as we got home, he saw Dr. Anju, and she told him he should have seen the ship's doctor; he could have made him more comfortable on the trip. He had not had any chemo for a long time, so she suggested that she give him a few treatments of a very strong drug. She added, "You've fought so hard I feel we should try one more thing." So, about a week later, she gave him his first injection of the powerful drug. She hoped this might give him a little more time if he could tolerate it.

One day, Gary walked into the room where I was and said, "I'm going to make you a sampler!" I told him I really would like that. Then he added, "I want you to promise you will not look at it until I'm gone." I promised. That would be easy for me; I have always tried to keep my word, and this was a special word I had given. So he would sit in the lounge chair on the porch or in the rocking chair in the room where I was sewing and work diligently making the cross-stitch sampler for me.

Sometime later he said, "I'm not going to be able to finish your sampler."

I expressed my regret and asked, "Is the message finished?"

He replied, "Yes, I've finished the message, but the decoration part isn't finished."

My answer was, "The message is the most important part, and I'll love it anyway, so don't worry about the fancy part."

Gary had always enjoyed taking candid photos at weddings for his friends and family, and he always did an excellent job. My grandson Earle was getting married in August of 1998, and he had asked Gary if he would do the candid shots, and he agreed. As time passed, however, I began to wonder if he would be able to go to

Columbia for the wedding. He had been in bed most of the time since the injection of the last chemo.

By this time, he had accepted that he was dying; and being a person who was always organized, he wanted to make his plans. Together we visited the funeral home, where he picked his casket and made plans for his funeral. I sat quietly by him as he went through this. I didn't feel it was my place to make any comments about how he wanted his life to end. He chose to be buried in the Veterans Cemetery near Bushnell, Florida, about forty miles from where we lived.

On our way home, I did ask him if he would do something special for me: to get the boat out of storage and take it to a place that sold them on consignment. So together we put all the boating accessories in the boat and towed it to the boat outlet. It was a very sad time for both of us. It sort of marked the end of our very special time together. I can say only that the person who bought the boat got a practically brand-new boat with all the accessories for a nominal price. I do hope whoever bought it enjoyed it as much as we did in the limited time we had to use it.

Now it was time for my grandson's wedding. It took only seven hours' driving time from our house to get to Columbia, and we usually made it in one easy day. This time I made arrangements for us to stop in Brunswick, Georgia, at the Hampton Inn for the night so Gary could rest. While he rested, I went outside and walked for many blocks around the motel.

The wedding was beautiful. Gary did take pictures, and they, too, were beautiful. At the reception, he wanted us to dance, but it was almost impossible for him to move. We did do one number, but it was so difficult for him that that ended our dancing. On our way back home, we stopped in Brunswick, Georgia, again for a night.

Soon it was time to return to Dr. Anju and receive a second injection of the strong chemo she was trying. He never said anything to me about what decision he had made, and I never asked. He was a very private person, and I respected that all the way. When we went in to see her, she talked to him, always, not me. He told her he had decided he did not want anymore chemo and told her how sick he had been. She asked if he'd made the wedding, and he perked up to tell her all about the pictures and how we did the trip. Then she told him she would refer him to hospice for the rest of his care.

Two men from Hospice of Citrus County, where we lived, came the next day and brought a hospital bed and other equipment we would need. Our bedroom was large, so I had the men put the hospital bed about two feet from the foot of our bed so we could easily move around to provide his care. Later, the nurse came to orient us to the service.

That night after everyone was gone, Gary called me and said, "Can I sleep with you tonight?"

"Of course you can. And any other time you feel the need to be beside me, just let me know." My daughter Ann, who is a nurse, had been with me for several days after Gary's condition had been determined, so she just stayed.

Early on, when Gary's cancer had been discovered and we learned how involved it was, I said to Dr. Anju, "I can't believe he doesn't have intense pain from this."

She said, "That doesn't happen until near the end."

The hospice nurse started him on morphine to make sure he was always comfortable, so he was quiet, sometimes sleeping and sometimes not. We had a grandfather clock, and at one point he asked me to stop the clock so he couldn't hear it.

Most of the time we just let him sleep. On Monday of his last week, he became lucid and asked if we had some of "that stuff," meaning Ensure, which I promptly prepared for him; he drank it all. Later he asked, "Do we have any chocolate ice cream?"

I replied, "Of course." So he ate a large serving of that; it was his favorite. He had lost so much weight that he really looked like a Holocaust victim.

Later the same day he said, "I have to keep fighting!"

I relied, "No, stop fighting. You've fought long and hard. Now it's time for you to close your eyes and go to sleep."

About two days later, Ann was sitting in the living room reading and she said, "I'll give Gary his twelve o'clock dose of morphine, so you can go to bed now. You can give the one early in the morning."

That sounded good to me; I was very tired, so I went to bed. All I could hear was the rhythmic sound of the oxygen being pumped to help him breathe easier.

Early the next morning, suddenly I was awakened because the rhythm was different. I jumped up quickly and saw Gary make about three shallow gasps and stop breathing. I hurried to get Ann, and we continued to check his pulse and found only negative signs. He ceased breathing at about 6:15 AM.

Very late in the evening, I cautiously picked up the sampler that Gary had been working on, and this is what it said:

TO: EMILY W. DAVENPORT "DOLL"

FROM: GARY JUNIOR DAVENPORT "LOVER"

I LOVE YOU DOLL. YOU ARE MY WIFE, MY LOVER, MY DRIVER, MY NURSE, MY NO. 1 PLAYMATE, AND MY VERY BEST FRIEND. I TRULY LOVE YOU.

The embroidery around the border was absolutely beautiful. The stitches were very intricate and perfect. Ann had added: DIED: 17 OCTOBER 1998.

What a wonderful gift!

When the hospice nurse visited, she had told me to call the hospice number when he expired. They have a nurse available twenty-four hours a day. I called and talked to the nurse, and she was there in about an hour. She called the funeral home, prepared Gary's body for the undertaker, and gathered all the leftover medications. A short time later, two men came and removed all the equipment. I take the time to tell you these details because it is a wonderful service, and it gave me so much comfort after carrying the burden alone for so long.

Gary died on Saturday morning, October 17, 1998, after six very long, hard years. Ann and I were very tired. On Sunday, I suggested that we drive to the National Cemetery so she could see where he would be buried. This cemetery is a beautiful, peaceful place and one of the best-maintained in the United States. Gary and I visited there many times just for the beauty of it. There are paths that meander beneath the trees and shrubs. It was on one of these visits that he told me he wanted to be buried there. He had disliked the extreme cold in the North and did not want to be buried there. Both of us had always been strong Christians, and we knew it really didn't matter where the body was buried, because the spirit was not there.

The funeral was held in our small Episcopal church, and there were friends standing all around the walls. They knew us well and were so supportive the entire time he was sick. When Gary planned his funeral, I was with him, and he stressed that he wanted the whole congregation to take Communion. This surprised me since he was reared in the Baptist church, but this is not foreign to Episcopalians. My daughter Ann sang "Amazing Grace" a cappella during Communion. Everything went just as Gary had planned it, and this was typical of the way he'd handled everything in his life.

I could not cry when he died. We had done that together for years, and he had planned it so well that I had already experienced closure. Now I could move on with my life, which is what he wanted for me. I did not know where I would live, but I did know that I didn't want to stay in Quail Run without him. Most of all, I wanted to be alone to rest for a while. My favorite way to be alone is to drive my car and listen to gospel tapes.

# Starting Over
## 1998-2000

I awoke one morning and decided I wanted to drive to San Diego, California, to see my childhood friend, Ella Ruth Fleming who had been in a nursing home with Parkinson's disease for years. She is the person I wrote about in the early part of this story. What a calming experience it was; I enjoyed every minute of it! We live in such a beautiful country that just seeing the varied landscapes can lift one's spirit.

When I returned home, I felt rested and more ready to decide my future. Gary had suggested that I move to Columbia, my home, so I made a trip up there to check out the housing opportunities. I was interested in a condo, but there were very few in Columbia at that time, none of which were right for me.

Ann suggested that I look for a condo in Naples, Florida, where she had been living since 1975. Knowing the wealth associated with Naples, I made the first trip to see if I could afford a condo that I would be willing to live in. I found several that would fit my requirements. I looked around the city and felt that I could be happy there, especially since I had a daughter there.

About a month later, I returned and found a lovely condo in a new development, and I was able to get a preconstruction price, which helped. The agent said it would be about a year before it would be completed. I thought it would take that long or longer to sell our house in Quail Run since it was semirural property. I committed to the condo on Friday and returned on Monday to make a down payment.

My neighbor Clayton Stetson, who had been so helpful to me when Gary was sick, asked about my trip to Naples. When I told him I had not only found a condo but had bought one at preconstruction price, he was very upset. He threw up all the usual "what if's": "What if your house doesn't sell? Property doesn't sell fast here. How will you be able to time it to fit the construction time table?"

I assured him that God had led me to that condo, and he would take care of me the same as he always had. I kept asking him, "Where is your faith?" So many people talk about faith but have a hard time living it. I knew it would all work out. But I had given the house to two realtors earlier, and they were not encouraging, so I let the contracts expire.

Home computers had been on the market for quite a while, but not many people had them. I'm sure you remember that Gary insisted that I have one, although he would not touch it. At first I used it like a word processor, but by this time I had signed up with Prodigy as my server. Prodigy had a lot of special offerings online, and one was real estate. On a whim, I put our house on their real estate site. A lady who lived near me called about our house, and I found out she was calling for a member of her family who was looking for a place close to her.

She told them about the house, and in about a week they came to see it. They were living in Hollywood, Florida, and wanted to get away from all the traffic and dense population in that area. They loved our house, it was just what they wanted, but they would have to sell their house first. In a short time, they sold their house for cash and paid me in cash; the title company prepared the paperwork; and it was all over. Clayton could not believe it, and I told him he must work on his faith!

Now that my house had been sold, I had to find a place to live. I put an ad in the county paper that read, "Single retired lady needs a temporary rental." I received a call the day the papers were delivered. Later I met a lady with her husband at the house, and she had a very interesting story. It seems that they owned about seven rental places, but they had just bought this one. They had never read the ads before, but somehow my ad just jumped out at them. I told them it could be as long as a year and explained my situation. We settled on $500 a month, and they would have the grass cut for me.

The house was in Beverly Hills, Florida, a nice development that was started in the 1950s with small houses like I had just rented. Many larger, more upscale houses have been built there in recent years. My place was on a corner lot, which was spacious and had a carport. The house had two bedrooms and one bath, but on the back a den had been added. It was perfect for storing the things that would go to Naples when my condo was completed. The house had been completely done over with new tile floors, carpet, and blinds, and all the walls had been newly painted. There were a new stove and refrigerator. The landlord had replaced the dryer, and she thought the washing machine could make it a while longer. When all of this is done to a masonry house, it's just like a brand-new house. As I told Clayton, "God didn't want me to be uncomfortable even for a short while."

A short time later, the washing machine flooded the laundry room, and I called the landlord. She told me, "Don't worry, Emily. I will send a new washer, and they will call you when it's time for delivery." I enjoyed my little house and always commented that it was so perfect for me that I would not mind staying as long as necessary. As it turned out, I was there for a year. You will never convince me that these things just happen. I know better.

Most of the little old houses were rentals, so there was a big turnover of occupants; most were low-income with lots of animals and children. Fences were not allowed. My neighbor Carolyn brought out food every night for the stray animals. One day, she told me about a little yellow cat that came every night for supper. Carolyn had a dog in the house, along with three cats and a husband on oxygen, and you know the size of the houses. After the cat had hung around for about two weeks, she said, "I just can't take this little cat to the pound. She would make someone a wonderful pet."

I replied, "I was going to wait until I went to Naples to get a cat, but I can take your little cat if you like." So now I had a yellow cat. Carolyn took her to the vet, who thought she was about a year old, and it took $500 to get her cleaned up. She had everything: pink eye, fleas, infected ears, worms, and everything else, so we assumed she had been on her own for a very long time. I paid the vet bill, and Carolyn came flying across the street with the litter pan and some food she had bought. That night, I put a bath towel on the foot of my bed. While talking to her, I patted the towel and said, "Now this is your bed. Come on, get on your bed." She jumped right up on the towel. I know she'd had a home at one time, because she had been spayed. How she came to be on her own we will never know, but she is one of my treasures. Carolyn was right: she has made a wonderful pet. I called her Goldie, because Carolyn had given her that name.

Even though I no longer attended the Methodist church in Inverness, I continued to meet with the United Methodist Women's group. They had become very good friends, and I still stay in touch with two of them. When I went to one of their meetings, a woman named Beverly was really upset. Her husband had recently had a stroke, and the doctor told her she would never be able to take him home. She never did like Florida, so she planned to take him home to New Hampshire. Bob would be flown to Boston with an aide, but Beverly was very concerned about getting her car to New Hampshire. I assured her that I would drive her car to New Hampshire for her, and she was greatly relieved.

In July of 2000, it was time for me to move into my condo in Naples. The movers picked up my things, I put Goldie in her carrier, and away we went to Naples. Once everything was unloaded, I went to The Cracker Barrel in Naples for lunch. When I was leaving, I talked to the cashier and expressed my concern that I had not been able to find a kennel for Goldie; I had to leave her to go out of town for five days. In fact, I was leaving that day. The lady said, "I know where you can leave Goldie—just give me a few minutes." She went into the back room, and soon she returned with the name and address of a kennel near where she lived. I received directions and took Goldie to the kennel.

I took a quick shower and left all the boxes from the move sitting in the middle of the floor. I drove back to Beverly Hills, where I had made arrangements with a neighbor to leave my car in her driveway while I drove Beverly's car to New Hampshire. Beverly and I stayed in a motel that night and left for New Hampshire the next morning. We were on the road for three days and had a wonderful time together. I caught a shuttle to the Boston airport and flew back to Tampa, picked up my car, and finally arrived at my condo. Beverly and I still stay in touch, and she will be ninety-four years old this year.

It was a good feeling to finally get into my condo in Briarwood, even though I'd been satisfied in the little house in Beverly Hills. What I really liked about the condo was how bright it was. It was that way because the living room, dining area, and kitchen had five windows, and there was a sliding glass door to the small screened porch. It was built according to a very compact plan. The master bedroom and the rooms I just mentioned were all at the back of the house, overlooking a small lake. The entrance was on the side but toward the back of the building. I had three bedrooms, but I used one for an office/library, and there was a single garage. I lived there for seven years, and the condo was most comfortable.

I went about unpacking the boxes and familiarizing myself with the community. I wanted to get involved to make friends and fill my spare time. First, I went to the hospital. After interviewing me, they assigned me to work in the Resource Center/Senior Center. I met a lot of friendly people, but the Center closed, because it did not support itself financially. I volunteered there for six months.

St. Paul Episcopal Church was close by, but because a gated community had its entrance just across the street from ours, it was necessary to go out of the way to get there.

Ann sang in the choir in another Episcopal church, but it was much farther away. She had been attending her church for more than thirty years. I felt it would be to my advantage to attend the one nearby in case it became necessary for someone to take me to church. Usually a large percentage of the members live in the area around the church. That was my rationale; but, in retrospect, I suspect I was sent there.

It didn't take me long to realize that this church was dying. There was a supply priest when I joined, and I thought that was probably the reason the members were falling away. Ann, whose church had started St. Paul's, said everybody knew about the problems there. But she had not told me. I decided I would attend until a permanent priest was found, and, if it looked like there was hope, I would work to try to build up the membership.

It had been several Sundays since I first attended St. Paul's, and on this particular Sunday, we were having a baptism. The priest called all the children to the front to stand around the font so they could see the baby. As we were going through the service and the priest was reading from the prayer book, I felt a tap on my shoulder. When I turned around, an older man asked, "Where is he reading from?"

I didn't want to talk to him and disturb the service, so I motioned to him and quietly said, "Come up here by me, and I'll show you." I was not quite at the end of the pew, so he slipped around and sat by me. We continued to read the service together.

After the service, he told me he had severe hearing problems, and then he began to cry, with big tears running down his face. He told me his wife of many years had died a few months earlier. I felt so bad for him; I told him I was coming to church alone and he could sit with me on Sunday so I could help him follow the service. In the Episcopal church, if you can't follow the prayer book, you are lost. He thanked me, and I left the church and thought no more about it.

Sure enough, the next Sunday he sat by me and for many more Sundays after that. One Sunday after church, we sat in the prayer garden and talked for a while; when he asked me if I would have lunch with him, I accepted. I could tell that he was very lonely and really needed someone to talk to. This was the beginning of a lovely friendship that lasted for four years.

We often talked about how we met with me just moving to Naples and him tapping me on the back, which was out of character for him. Even stranger was the fact that he had been an Episcopalian much longer than I. He wanted to talk about his wife and told me about her lung problems, how he tried to look after her, and how surprised the family was when she died at that particular time.

Another ironic thing was that my education major was in exceptional children, and I had studied hearing loss and the use of hearing aids. He told me he had 95 percent hearing loss in each ear. At that time, I wore a microphone for conversation, and the hearing loss did not bother me at all.

# A New Friend

## 2000-2004

His name was Merton, and he was two years older than I. I knew he had lots of problems, but I had spent my adult life working with people with problems, so it was nothing new to me. When people reach their eighties, they know there isn't much more time to enjoy their lives. I remembered the vow I'd made when I was seventeen: that I would spend the rest of my life trying to make things better for others. This included helping Mert to have a better life in the time he had left.

Mert told me that his two children wanted to take him away from Naples now that his wife had died, but they had been in Naples since 1989, and he did not want to leave. Later, I told his children that if they would let him stay in Naples, I would look out for him. If he became sick, I would see that he went to his doctor; and if there were any major changes in his health, I would let them know right away. I guess they could tell I was sincere, because they gave up trying to move him.

After about two years, he began having difficulty taking care of his pool and very large house. I suggested that he consider selling his house and moving into a facility that provided independent living. He knew the house was too much for him, so he agreed to consider it.

He discussed selling the house with his children, and they agreed that he should put it on the market. One of his neighbors contacted him and offered to buy the house. In the meantime, Mert and I visited several assisted-living places in Naples I had visited before. He looked them over, got information, and then decided which one he liked best.

Mert and his son, Jeff, sold the house to his neighbor, and he moved into Merrill Gardens in Naples, which is an assisted-living place, but he would live independently. He chose this facility, and I agreed with him that it should meet his needs.

A permanent priest was selected by the search committee for St. Paul's. After he had been there for a year, nothing had changed, and I'm not sure it had not worsened. I was not happy with the situation.

An announcement was made at the church a volunteer was needed to take the altar flowers to the hospital each Sunday. I asked Mert if he would like to help me, and he agreed, so we delivered the flowers for a year. We were told that the names of the patients would be given to us. Yes, they were—for the first Sunday. From then on, I would ask anyone I thought should know, but no one ever did. Then, "I made a way". I had a list of shut-ins, my telephone and a Naples map. We would pick up the flowers, call a shut-in and deliver the flowers and it worked well.

The churches in Naples have Saturday services during the winter months. I suggested that we go to the Episcopal church on Saturday and visit a Methodist church on Sunday. We visited North Naples United Methodist Church, which had about two thousand members. We liked it immediately. Mert did not grow up in a church, but his wife was Episcopalian, so that's why he became an Episcopalian. Later, he wanted to join the Methodist church with me; we joined, and he attended there for a couple of years.

We joined the church in August, and I was contacted by one of Mert's friends, Charlotte Roe, that the board of the United Methodist Women would like to interview me for the presidency for the next two years. I was floored. I asked Charlotte, the caller, "How do they know about me?"

She said, "I had been with you and Mert when he invited me to go to lunch with you. As soon as I saw you, I knew you were the right person!"

Remember, I had been an Episcopalian for the prior ten years. I really knew nothing about the United Methodist Women, but I said to myself that I had done all kinds of things, so surely I could handle a church group. God again had put me where he wanted me to be.

The board asked me all about my life but the members were most concerned about my faith. You have to remember that I had just walked in off the street, so to speak. Usually, active members just move up, and everyone knows them. There I was a total stranger about whom they knew nothing. I doubt that anyone else has ever had to interview for that volunteer position.

I sat in on two board meetings and met the officers. What I found out was that in the previous year there had been a big screaming match among some ladies, and the whole church had been upset. It had been a terrible verbal fight, and I could not believe that such a thing could take place in a church group. But I could fix that. I knew how to work with women.

I met privately with the ring leader of each side of the issue. I told them they would not serve on any committees during the next year, and I would not discuss the problem anymore, and neither would they.

At the first board meeting, they saw that I could lead and that I meant what I said. I told them, "I am well aware of what happened last year, but that's over; and it is, as of now, forgotten. If you start anything like that again, you will have to look for another president, because I will resign." Throughout my career, I'd had to handle conflict of all kinds, and they could see that. They had never had a professional person leading before. We had two outstanding years together. They were a fine group of women, but it does take a strong leader.

One of our pastors, a lovely lady, told me, "I have been in this church for eight years, and I have never seen the women so happy!"

I really worked those two years, but I enjoyed it and learned so much about volunteer workers. I started with six groups or Circles with 160 women but ended with seven Circles and 175 women. It was a fun time.

One day, while reading the paper, I read that there was a great need for literacy volunteers. I took the course and tutored one man for about four months. When he moved, I tutored a girl for three months, until she changed jobs and no longer had time to be tutored. The last person was a man who had a lovely wife and a twelve-year-old son. They were from Colombia, South America. He worked at our church as a janitor and was taking courses at the community college. I tutored him until I left Naples.

*** 

I had been attending the Self Help for the Hard of Hearing (SHHH) organization with Mert all the time we were friends. He had been reading and learning all he could about getting a cochlea implant to improve his hearing. There were two places in Florida where this would be possible, Miami or Sarasota. We chose Sarasota, and he had the surgery on one ear. The surgery was successful, and he was so pleased to actually be able to hear again. The programming of the implant required a lot of follow-up, so for several months we made many trips to Sarasota from my house, a journey of one hundred miles each way.

About two years after the surgery, I noticed that Mert was not hearing as well as before. At the next scheduled appointment, I didn't tell the audiologist about my concern; I wanted to see if she found the same thing when he was tested in the silent room. She reported that the device was working perfectly, but he was not processing, which is a sign of a brain problem. I really don't think Mert ever realized what her interpretation was. I didn't mention it, so we continued as before. Nothing could be done to correct the problem.

At this time, Mert was driving to my house at about 3:00 PM each day, and I prepared supper for us or we went out. We would visit and watch TV, and he would return to Merrill Gardens before they locked up at 9:00 PM. His dementia became serious suddenly. I told him that he must not drive anymore; it was not safe for him or others. For a while, I drove to Merrill Gardens, picked him up, took him to my condo for supper, and then drove him back, but I knew I could not continue to do this every day.

It was time for me to keep my promise, so I wrote an email to his children and explained what had happened. In a few days, his son Jeff came. More testing was done, which confirmed what we already knew.

His daughter Janet, who lived in New York, invited him to come up for Labor Day for a visit. He did not want to go, but I encouraged him to go to visit with his grandchildren. When I went to pick him up to go to the airport, he came out with no luggage. He had forgotten that he was supposed to be going to New York. I went in to get his one bag, checked it, and found that he had practically nothing in it. I quickly packed his clothes and took him to the airport.

Mert's Janet, who is a physician, would not let him return to Naples as planned. I felt that I had betrayed him, because I had encouraged him to go for a visit. We all knew that this was the best thing for him, but he grieved because he wasn't with me. In late October, and again just before Christmas, I went up for a visit to help him accept the new living arrangements. He lived in a small apartment in a retirement hotel, which was very nice, and his family had secured a medical aide to be with him all day every day. He and I had communicated by email from the time we met, because he couldn't talk on the telephone, and we continued to do that until he was no longer able.

Mert was a lovely gentleman, and we enjoyed each other. We spent a lot of time talking about our early lives and "how it used to be," World War II, and the things we both had been a part of during a very important time in the history of the United States. We never talked about money; we weren't interested in that. I wanted to fulfill my vow, and he really needed someone to help him grieve for his wife and enjoy the later years of his life. When he came to my house in the evenings, I would ask him what he wanted for supper; then we would go to the store and buy what we needed, and I would prepare it. When we went out to eat, he always picked up the check. When we traveled, I kept a running account of the expenses, and each of us paid half. I always drove, and I just thought I would throw that in free since I get so much pleasure from it myself.

I really missed Mert terribly, but I tried to encourage him to accept the fact that he was where he needed to be at this point in his life. He loved Naples, the Naples he knew when he and his wife had moved there. Growing old is extremely difficult. For years, a couple works to build a life together and rear a family. They are the center of their universe. But the time comes when this couple is pushed aside, and they no longer have any say about anything, not even their own lives. But that's the way it will always be as one generation moves out and another moves in. Neither generation understands the other, because nothing stays the same. I learned very early in my education that "the only thing constant is change." As the population grows and longevity increases, there will be a big question to answer. What will we do with the old so the young can assume their rightful place in society? I'm afraid the decision will be very painful for those living when that time comes.

Mert had been attending the Episcopal church while he was in New York. He died on January 19, 2007. His ashes are interred beside his wife's in Chicago, Illinois.

# A Painful Episode
## 2005-2006

The next year, after Mert moved to New York, something else happened that would change things again for me. At this point, Ann was working in Perth, Australia, and was to be there for two years before she came home. She called me one night, very upset, and told me that her son Arthur was in desperate circumstances. Arthur had been running a night club in Orlando, Florida, for several years, and he had been very successful. I had seen him several times since I had been living in Naples. But somehow, as we all know now, it is very easy for people to get into drugs. Arthur, who was thirty-three years old, had lost his job and his beloved BMW, and his wife had thrown him out of their home. He had no money and nowhere to go, and his mother was very, very far away. Ann asked me if he could come to Naples and stay with me until he could get himself straightened out. My reply was, "Of course he can. He's my grandson." She sent him a ticket to fly from Orlando to Fort Myers. His plane was late but finally arrived at about 11:30 PM.

Arthur, who was a handsome young man, came up the jetway carrying in his arms the computer he had built himself. Earlier in his life, he'd been tested, and his IQ was 145. He looked terrible. I went to meet him, put my arms around him, and told him everything would be okay and that I loved him very much. He seemed to feel better as we picked up the small bag he'd brought with him. He had no clothes.

After we arrived at my condo, I put him and all he had in my guest room. I urged him to bathe and go to bed. Tomorrow would be early enough to sort out the situation.

Arthur had never met a stranger. He was friendly to everyone, and he made friends easily. In his job, he'd been exposed to all-night activities; and, with his personality, it's easy to see how he could get into trouble, even as intelligent as he was. I had not been around him since he became an adult, so I really didn't know how things would be with him living with me.

The next morning, I told him, "Arthur, I am an old woman, and I have been living alone for seven years. While you stay with me, you will live by my rules, or you will have to leave; and I don't think you have anywhere to go. So you don't have much choice. But we will set up a way to get you back on your feet, and we will work together to accomplish it. Do you accept these stipulations?" He did.

Drugs were no mystery to him. He knew all about how to use them and how to recover, so he could do it over and over. I learned that he had done this at least twice before, so he was extremely knowledgeable. Sometime earlier, he had checked himself into a methadone clinic as a treatment for his drug dependency. Now he had to get off the methadone, which, he told me, would take a week to ten days.

The first thing I did was put him on vitamins and an adequate diet and get his clock "repaired." He would sleep at night and get up in the morning. This is not something that you can do suddenly; rather, it was to be a slow process. I prepared meals from scratch and made him get up and eat. The whole time he was with me, he behaved according to my plans.

For the first two weeks he was with me, things were pretty quiet, and he followed the regimen to the letter. But he told me he could go outside and get any drug he wanted in ten minutes. I insisted that he walk outside, and I went with him for quite a while. Gradually he began to improve, and he could always tell me exactly how the drug was leveling off in his body.

Soon he wanted us to go to the store and get him some clothes. He wanted to go to Ross's, and he went straight to the racks and picked his pants and then his shirts. Remember, he had no money. The clothes he bought were certainly not the quality he had been used to wearing, but this was where he chose to go. Now that I had bought him some clothes, we could go out to eat and see a movie. In fact, we had a really good time together.

He went to church and Sunday school with me every Sunday after the first couple of weeks, and he told me how much he enjoyed it. We sat for hours talking about his condition, drugs, and religion, among other topics. I bought him a Bible, and we discussed various parts of the scriptures.

Around the first of January, he was ready to look for a job. He liked to cook and had worked in a restaurant when he was in high school. He wanted to try to find a restaurant job. He visited three or so, and everywhere he went they wanted to hire him. He really looked good; looking at him, one would never suspect what he had been through.

He walked into an upscale restaurant in Naples, and the owner saw him and came over to talk to him. This was a man Arthur had trained to run a nightclub when he was running the club in Orlando. Of course, the man hired him on the spot. He hurried home to get his white chef's jacket, and I took him back to start work that day.

Arthur had no way to get to work, and he would not get off until about 11:00 PM. We talked about this, and both of us realized I could not provide transportation every day. I suggested that he find a used car, and his mother and I would buy it for him. But this young man was used to having a BMW and the best of everything, so he would not consider a used car. He thought the best idea was for him to get a motorcycle. He'd had cycles over the years; in fact, he used to repair them. He could do anything he put his mind to. His mother did not like the idea, and certainly I didn't. But he won his argument.

I took Arthur to a man's house, where he bought a motorcycle. Ann stressed that this was only for transportation to work and back, and he agreed to that. All of these decisions were made with his mother, and I did not interfere. Ann came from Australia shortly after he had bought the motorcycle. I was very relieved when she returned; I didn't want the responsibility of making decisions for him.

Very soon after Ann returned to Naples, she told me she had to take Arthur to work. I asked about the motorcycle, and she told me he had wrecked it the day before. It seems that he'd been stopped at a red light, and when the light changed, the car in front of him did not move fast enough, so he rear-ended it. Of course, this bashed in the front of his bike, but he was able to ride it, even though it was not completely repaired.

Ann checked all around, trying to find Arthur a small condo that he and his buddy could share. She finally found one on a golf course that she could buy and use as an investment.

The first of March, six months after Arthur came to stay with me, he and his friend moved into the condo that Ann had bought for them. They would pay enough rent to cover the mortgage. Everything looked good, but I did not feel good about the situation. But Ann needed to get back to her job in Australia, so I thought I would just be there if Arthur needed me.

But God had another plan for me. I was going to my college reunion in Spartanburg, South Carolina, in the first part of April, and I was going to see two of my children in Columbia. I had felt that nudging that comes to me when God is directing me to do something he thinks is best for me. I had lunch with a friend, and I found myself telling her briefly about my situation. Ann was no longer in Naples, and Arthur was working and living in a condo, so there was no reason for me to stay in Naples. I felt I should return "home" to Columbia. She had brought a booklet with her that she thought I would like to review since I had lived there years before. I took the booklet back to my motel room.

Later, I picked up the booklet. It looked like it contained recipes, so I just causally leafed through it. On the back was a full-page ad about some new condos being built. They looked just like what I had wanted years earlier. These things do not just happen to me.

The next morning, I called the office of the realtor whose name was in the article. I asked if a certain man still worked there; he did, and she put him on the telephone. He'd grown up with my children, so I told him of my interest in the condos. He had not received the information yet, since the construction was brand new. He was able to get the information from the guy who would be on-site later. Then he said, "Let's drive over there so you can see the location." At that time, the site was only a bare field; not even a road had been put in. I looked at the plan, and the realtor helped me select the lot that would be best for me. The location was perfect—I couldn't have done better myself—and the price was one I could handle. I signed a commitment and gave him a check for a down payment. I had heard the message that it was time for me to return "home." When God tells me what to do, I never hesitate, because I know it is the right decision. He has never failed me!

I was very happy as I drove back to Naples. I was going "home," to a place I knew was right for me. My mind was going a hundred miles an hour as I thought about what I needed to do to sell my house. I had been given a video and all the information about the development, and I couldn't wait to tell my children. Later, when I did tell them, they were very disinterested. It was okay, sort of. I have always handled my own affairs.

About two weeks later, at 1:00 AM, my phone rang. When this happens, it is usually a wrong number, so I did not answer it; I let the answering machine take the message. I could hear my granddaughter's voice telling me that Arthur had had a serious accident and that he was in critical condition in the hospital in Fort Myers. I jumped out of bed. After she hung up, I called Ann, who was her mother also.

Ann was already on her way back to Australia but had stopped in Virginia to visit her older sister. She could not give me much detail, but a motorcycle was involved. She told me, "He might die, Mother!" I was devastated and asked if I should meet her at the airport, but she had already talked to a friend who would pick her up. As upset as I was, I was not surprised; I had gotten very familiar with Arthur's behavior.

\*\*\*

We learned later what had happened. After work at the restaurant, the young people were outside behind the building, where there was a guy who had an Italian motorcycle; he was trying to impress the workers. He had been having some trouble with the bike, and he told the others he was going to take it to a shop to be fixed. Arthur, with his knowledge of motorcycles, asked if he could check it; perhaps he could repair it for him and save him some money. He climbed on the bike and gave it the gas, and it took off fast. Arthur could not stop it or get off as it sped ahead and drove him into a concrete wall. He was not wearing a helmet. He was air-lifted to the critical care unit at the hospital in Fort Myers.

He was immediately put on life support, and he lived for eleven days. Ann's longtime friends rallied around her, and some members of our family came to Fort Myers. My condo was the headquarters; visitors came and brought all kinds of food for the family, and I kept up with the things necessary for daily living. I would listen to their reports: some days better, some not as good. I visited the hospital once and looked at the handsome grandson I had worked so hard to "heal," and I knew his life was over.

After ten days, the family agreed to take him off life support. At ten o'clock the next day, he stopped breathing.

Arthur's memorial service was held in the beautiful Episcopal church in Naples, and an unknown member of the church paid for some of Arthur's ashes to be buried in the garden space outside the church. Ann put in some ashes and then handed me the trowel so I could also put in some of the ashes. Later, the rest of the ashes were taken by boat to one of the Florida Keys and cast into the water. It was a place where the family liked to go scuba diving. A few months later, Ann returned to Australia.

Our all-knowing God knew the future and knew what was going to happen. He did not want me to be in Naples alone, so far from the rest of my family. As always, he loves me and takes care of me, and all the rest just falls into place.

I have played the piano all my life and enjoyed it. Most of the time I was playing, I had a small child on my lap. Ann majored in music in college, and she dreamed of having a concert grand piano. Finally, at some point she was able to buy a beautiful piano just like she wanted. When she went to Australia the first time, she asked me to keep her piano for her. Now that was something I was thrilled to do. For the first year, I played about an hour a day to get back into practice. Katy, my oldest daughter, who heard me play at that time, said I played as well as I had when she was in high school. That piano was a delight to play, and I played regularly.

Later, Ann bought a townhouse in Atlanta for herself and her daughter Emily. And guess what? She wanted to take her piano back. She told me she had a Spinet in storage, and I could have that one. I was glad to get it, but it wasn't the same.

Since Arthur died, I have not played much at all. I like to play when I'm happy, and so far I haven't felt happy like I did several years ago. I still have the Spinet with me, and when I get really happy, I'll play again. Arthur's death was especially hard for me.

After I had made all the arrangements to build a condo in Lexington, South Carolina, I had returned to Naples. I told my friend Nora about it. She came to my house to see the video and look at the floor plans. She was so excited and asked, "How can I get one, too?"

I asked, "Have you ever been to South Carolina?"

She answered, "No, but if you're going, I want to go with you." I told her to call them and send a check for $1000, and they would be glad to let her have one. I was surprised, but she did call and bought a condo like mine.

We made three trips to Lexington during the construction, and I drove Nora around the area. We selected all the things necessary for a new house, and each time we went up, we were very happy with the place. I wanted to get some new furniture; I had been using the furniture Gary had brought from Chicago when we married. I reasoned that this would probably be my last house, so I wanted some things that I would choose and that would make the condo really mine.

Meanwhile, the housing market nationwide seemed to be in trouble. Real estate prices that had been too inflated were beginning to drop. I put my condo in Naples on the market, and the agent set the price in line with others in the complex. I suggested we price it lower; it had to sell.

One day in November, a realtor brought a nice-looking young man to look at the condo. About two days later, he came back alone and asked if he could come in and talk to me. He realized it was a "no no" for him to come without his agent. But I invited him in, and we talked. He said, "I really do want your house."

And I replied, "And I really want you to have my house."

He had just returned after being deployed to the war in Iraq. He would be getting a GI loan, and he couldn't pay what I was asking. I told him I was not trying to make any money off the sale. But I did want to be able to pay for my move and the things I would need, such as window treatments and some furniture. I suggested that he let me do some figuring on the money. I would cut it as close as I could, and I would let him know. In February, the two realtors came again, and I ended up lowering the price by $50,000. He was so pleased, and I was so happy for him. I received enough money to do what I wanted to do. Again, God was there telling me what I should do, and I had such a good feeling about it. I've never missed the money.

Soon it was moving day. I had taken my cats to the vet's office for the night. Oh, I don't think I've told you, but now I had a second cat. Two years after I got Goldie, she started biting me and not acting as she usually did. Ann told me she was used to being outside and was bored being indoors all the time; she said I should get her a kitten. I got her a little gray tabby; he was only eight weeks old and very small. I named him Lil' Boy, but officially he is B.C., which stands for Boy Cat. Ann thought that was a terrible name, but I liked it, and now when I call "Lil' Boy," he comes running. What a joy he is! The two cats love each other.

The next morning, we started our journey to Lexington, South Carolina, which is 650 miles from Naples, too far for one day. We stopped in Brunswick, Georgia, for the night. I just had to laugh. I went inside and brought out the luggage cart, which I loaded with cat food, three bowls, cat litter, litter pan, and beds. Then I picked up my tiny carry-on and a purse. Later I told my friends that it was like travelling with two-year-old twins. The cats were so good, but they did not want the radio turned on in the car. That was okay; I sang to them.

When we arrived where the condo was being built, I was told it was not ready, and it would be several weeks before it would be. They sent me to an extended-stay hotel that took pets, and we unloaded again. It was a very nice room, with a king-sized bed, mini-kitchen, bath, and living area. We were there for a month, and I didn't find it bad at all. It gave me time to get some rest I really needed. My furniture was put into storage, and some things have never shown up, but that's the casualty of moving.

Everything appeared to be going fine for us at the extended-stay hotel until the maid came to clean the unit. I was not there. She brought in a large commercial vacuum cleaner that made an extremely loud noise, and it scared Goldie to death. After that, I stayed home to hold her in the hall when the cleaning lady came. Everything about the move made Goldie feel endangered, and it took a year to get her feeling comfortable again. I have read that environment is very important to cats, but, strange as it seems, Lil' Boy did just fine.

I understand about the environment for cats. I have a large double garage that opens into the back hall. Each morning and afternoon both cats go into the garage and walk all the way around my car and come back in. They are making sure no one has bothered our "stuff". I had never had indoor cats before, but I can tell you it is very different from having cats that go outside. They have a routine they do every day. They know everything I say to them and they also know my routine. I would be lost without them.

Finally, my condo was finished and we moved our stuff in. My new furniture was delivered, and the other things were unpacked. The condo is so spacious, and new things always look so good. I gave thanks every day that I had been able to purchase this new place, sell my house in Florida, make the move, and get settled, and I did most of it alone. Ann came and helped me in Lexington. We are so much alike that when she set up everything in my kitchen cabinets,

I would reach out for something and it was there. Sarah Jane came to help for a short while as well.

Nora's condo was finished before mine, so she had been busy learning her way around; but when I got moved in, we did many things together. She had heard about a great United Methodist church in Lexington that was growing by leaps and bounds. We decided we would visit. After church, we went out to eat and discussed the church. She said, "Well, what do you think about it?"

I answered, "Let's wait and see what they think about us!"

Later in the afternoon, a man came to deliver a fresh loaf of bread to each of us. On Monday, one pastor phoned me, and on Tuesday, another one called. So I told Nora, "Well, I guess they'd like to have us join them!" And we did.

The next Sunday, we attended a Sunday school class that we selected from the brochure. It was perfect for us, mostly older people whom we have come to love. When we first walked in, a lady looked at me and said, "I know you!"

And I replied, "Yes, and I know you, too!" She had worked in the school district where I'd worked years before, but each of us had remarried and had different names.

As usual, I became involved right away. I had taken the Stephen Ministry course in Naples. It is a lay ministry, and the training takes fifty hours. The course prepares the person to be a "friend" to someone else who is going through a crisis situation. It is an excellent program. I have had a retired nurse's license for many years, but I wanted this training so I could visit church members and represent our church.

I had worked with the congregational care minister in Naples, so I made an appointment to meet the person responsible for congregational care at Mt. Horeb, where Nora and I had just joined. I had prepared a brief resume. He suggested that I visit the extended care facility once a week. Our church had three residents there, but when I visited a semiprivate room and prayed with our church member, the person in the other bed said, "Will you pray for me, too?" Of course I did. I have been doing this for two years every

Wednesday, and the people there look for me every week. It is most rewarding. It helps me as much as, or more than, it does them.

It has been perfect for me to work with older people. Since I am older myself, I can identify with everything they tell me about themselves. There have been so many times that I've said to myself, *Mother, now I understand what you were trying to tell me.* But as a young person, I didn't have a clue. No one generation can ever fully understand another because of the changes that take place as one slowly grows older and different parts of the body begin to break down. Young people think they are invincible and will live forever. That's the reason why trying to teach disease prevention to teenagers often fails.

# A Very Old Friend Shows Up!
## 2008-2010

Just before Christmas of 2008, my telephone rang. When I answered, a man said, "Is this Emily?"

"Yes, it is."

"Do you know a Jack Turney?"

"No, I knew a Turney man a long time ago, but his name was not Jack."

"Was it Raymond Bruce?"

"Oh, my gosh! Is that you?"

I could not believe it. It had been sixty-eight years since I had seen or heard from him. We talked for about two hours, just catching up. He is the founder and president of The Spoken Word of God Ministries and president of International Christian Media, Company. Both are located in Orlando, Florida. When I moved back to South Carolina, I sent a small notice to our school paper, and his daughter, who works for him, found my phone number on the Internet. I had worded it using "I," so he knew I was alone. He told me he wanted to celebrate the Fourth of July at his mountain home in North Carolina. He said the scenery was so beautiful, and it is. R. B. has a wife, who is sick with Alzheimer's, and they have three adult children.

After he talked to me, he sent me some printed material about his ministries and included some DVDs that I thoroughly enjoyed.

It was all very interesting, and I was glad to know about his work. He included some grapefruit from his trees in the package. That was sort of a bonus.

Some weeks later, R. B. came by to see me, and we had vegetable soup and cornbread on my sun porch. It was great to just sit and talk about our families and our careers. Of course, we looked a bit different from the way we looked a long time ago, but we had no difficulty sharing our life experiences.

Another time, R. B. was coming to see me, and he called from about seventy-five miles away, where he was speaking, to say he would not to be able to make it. He was having a terrible headache, and he did not know why. I was concerned since he was planning to go to India in a few weeks. Early one morning, when I had my devotionals, I had a very strong feeling that he should not go to India. I called his cell phone and left him a message. "I just wanted to tell you, before you go to India, please see your doctor."

I did not hear anything for several weeks, but when he called, he sounded terrible; I could barely understand him. I asked what was wrong. He said, "I just got out of the hospital. I was there for two weeks. The doctor had to put in a pacemaker." I was glad I had asked him to see his doctor. He did not go to India. It was a disappointment for him, but he knew it was best.

Before long, R. B. came by and brought Joshua, an Indian pastor, with him. They were expected around 10:30 AM, and we talked until they left at 3:00 PM. I said, "If I had known you were going to be here this long, I would have prepared lunch for you!" Joshua told me that R. B. kept falling asleep driving, and he had to keep him awake. Joshua does not drive. They were headed for a six- or eight-state tour to raise money, but again, I was concerned about him driving. We talked about it, but they were going to the mountain place first. Later, I called Ann, who is a surgical nurse, you remember, and she said his pacemaker needed to be adjusted. She has had more experience with heart matters than I have. The next time I talked to him, his doctor had adjusted his pacemaker, and he was doing much better; but he thought the pacemaker might need some more adjusting.

I am now in the third week of June, and R. B. called me to remind me that I was to go with them to the mountains for July Fourth. The arrangements have been made for Goldie and Lil' Boy, and I'm looking forward to the trip.

I have not travelled much since moving back to South Carolina; I don't like to leave my "family," Goldie and Lil' Boy. They are wonderful pets. The best part is that they always agree with me. I lead a very busy life, and I wouldn't swap it for anything. God has been so good to me! He cares for me, and he cares for you!

# What's Next? Who Knows?

## 2009-?

I don't know what will happen to me next, but you can be sure of one thing: whatever it will be, it will be wonderful and just another adventure. Life is for living, and I can honestly say I have lived it to the fullest. God isn't through with me yet!

If you look in the 1941 annual for Textile Industrial Institute (now Spartanburg Methodist College), you will see my picture, and beneath the picture is written, "I'll try to find a way, and if I can't, I will make one!" Very appropriate, don't you think?

Emily W. Davenport, June 20, 2009

# Index

LaVergne, TN USA
21 January 2011
213342LV00002B/9/P